THE ORIGINS

The Ages of Mathematics

VOLUME ONE

THE ORIGINS

Michael Moffatt

DOUBLEDAY & COMPANY, INC.
GARDEN CITY, NEW YORK

510.9
A265
v. 1
c-1

7-77
5.95

ISBN 0-385-11214-9 TRADE
0-385-11215-7 PREBOUND
LIBRARY OF CONGRESS CATALOG CARD NUMBER 76–10336
PRINTED IN THE UNITED STATES OF AMERICA
FIRST EDITION

CONTENTS

1

IN THE BEGINNING

In primitive societies, the first simple mathematical developments were prompted by practical necessities. Even the pre-monetary system of barter required some method of counting (if you barter three sheep for six bags of corn, you still have to be able to count them). And the earliest method was what mathematicians now call "one-to-one correspondence"—one finger representing one sheep, two fingers two sheep, etc. It is not at all surprising that fingers and toes were the earliest "adding machines" in use. And also perhaps they were the basis for the later adoption of our system of counting in tens.

The sense of number is not limited to human beings. Birds, in particular, seem to have some limited "number sense." An animal psychologist developed an experiment in which birds were given rewards of food for being able to recognize specific numbers of dots. He provided for two ways of counting the numbers, one in which all of the dots were shown simultaneously, and one in which they were presented one after another. Results showed that certain species of birds did recognize numbers of dots, up to certain limits. Pigeons could keep track of up to five or six dots; jackdaws recognized six; and ravens and parrots seven. There are reports from hunters that crows seem to be able to differentiate between numbers up to four or five—but these were not controlled experiments.

Among people, number sense, or at least the capacity for describing numbers, seems to vary considerably. Thus, you can talk about twenty or thirty or one hundred objects, or about the twentieth or thirtieth or hundredth, and probably have a pretty good idea of what you are talking about. More primitive people living a less complicated life are not so specific. In the language of one South American tribe, for example, there are but five number words:

> *pemi*—indicating "none"
> *moni*—one or a few, but not as many as *nami*
> *carekep*—two or more than one, but not as many as *carami*
> *carami*—many, usually five or more

And when you stop and think about how often you use "few," "several," "many," and words of the kind, it is not too difficult to imagine situations in which five number words are adequate. The Tsimshian Indians of British Columbia, for example, have seven sets of words to describe numbers: 1) flat objects and animals; 2) round objects and time; 3) men; 4) long objects; 5) canoes; 6) measures; and 7) counting without direct reference to objects. A Tsimshian Indian might well be confused by a *pair* of gloves, a *couple* of people, a *team* of horses, *twins*, or a *brace* of birds, not to mention tennis doubles.

As cultures become more complex, their involvement with numbers becomes correspondingly complicated. For example, a primitive goatherd might keep count of his goats by using one rock to represent one goat. He would find that a number of small piles of rocks are easier to cope with mentally, if not physically, than is one big pile. And, if you put the same number of stones in each small pile, the organization is still easier. Now, how many rocks should you put in each small pile? That is, to what base would you develop your number system?

The favorites throughout the world have been "five," "ten," and "twenty." It seems safe to assert that the choice of these bases is related to the biological fact that most individuals have five fingers to each hand, two hands, and two feet, each complete with five toes.

There is some evidence for this conjecture in some languages. The Zuñi, for example, describe:

"one" as "taken to start with"
"two" as "put down together with"
"three" as "the equally divided fingers"
"four" as "all the fingers but one done with"
"eight" as "three brought to and held up with the rest"
"ten" as "all the fingers"
"twenty" as "all the fingers two times"
"one hundred" as "all the fingers of all the fingers."

But even so simple a notion as finger counting and grouping can be complicated by different interpretations. In fact, if you ask a number of people how many fingers they have on each hand, you will find that at least one of these people will say "four fingers and one thumb." And there you have the beginnings of a number system based on four. There is an example of this in one New Guinea tribe. They count:

1. . . . ."one"
2. . . . ."two"
3. . . . ."three"
4. . . . ."hand"
5. . . . ."thumb"
6. . . . ."two thumbs"
7. . . . ."three thumbs"
8. . . . ."two hands"
9. . . . ."two hands, one thumb"
10 . . . ."two hands, two thumbs"
11 . . . ."two hands, three thumbs"
12 . . . ."three hands"

and, not surprisingly, at "twenty" you find that "feet" get into the act. The "three thumbs" and "three hands" may be a bit puzzling, but scholars may find in their use the beginnings of a capacity for abstractions.

In Finno-Ugric, the language family to which Finnish and Hungarian belong, the words for the first five numbers are simple, while that for six is complicated. Though the number system of these people is now based on ten, it is thought that originally it was based on six, with the five fingers taken as the first five numerals, and the whole hand considered separately as the sixth.

In all of this research on word origins there is a great deal of speculation. And, however objective the researcher-speculator, there is the possibility that his conclusions may reflect some of his own prejudices. For example, a person who believes that the most reasonable base for a number system is a prime number (just for the record, a prime number is one that is divisible only by itself and one—2, 3, 5, 7, etc.) might look at these same Finno-Ugric number-words and note that the word for seven is also a complex one, while those for eight and nine are composite (in the same sense that thirteen is "composite"—three and ten) and argue that the number base in those languages must have been seven. And in many cultures there *is* something special, even mystical, about the number seven.

There is an analogue to this in the English number-words. You count up to twelve, and then you come to the composite words, thirteen, fourteen, and so on. Suppose you were dedicated to the idea that twelve is the most reasonable base for a number system. Might you not look upon these words as evidence to support your argument? And, then you could point to the wide use of "dozen" and, though perhaps less widely, "gross" (twelve multiplied by twelve) as additional evidence. If there are people five thousand years from now interested in such propositions, they might just make these arguments. They could also point to the business of dividing the foot into twelve inches as further evidence in favor of their hypothesis.

The study of word origins, in general, is quite a fascinating and complex business. For example, there are the Indo-European root words for the smaller number-words of many languages—Greek, Latin, German, English, French, Russian—with their original meanings:

Number	Indo-European Root	Original Meaning
1	oi	"this here"
2	du	"that there"
3	ter	"over, beyond"

That is, there may have been a time when, instead of simply holding up two fingers or naming the second finger to express the numeration of, say, two horses, a man would say something like "this horse here and that horse there." "Beyond," as distinct from "over there," gave the system a third element. For three horses, then, that man might say: "this horse and that horse and the horse beyond."

On the other hand, there are some rather obvious causes for speculation on number-word origins. In present-day Indo-European languages, the words for the smaller cardinal and ordinal numbers are dissimilar, while those for the larger are closely related. In the English, for instance:

Cardinal	Ordinal
one	first
two	second
three	third
four	fourth

and so on. Apparently, when the ancient Indo-Europeans were dealing only in terms of "one," "two," and "many," they didn't associate the idea of "how many" with order—first and second.

Ironically, certain of our English number-words—
"hundred" and "thousand," among others—do not give a clue
to the most important number development, from a mathematical point of view, anyway—that of positional notation.

For example, primitive man may have found it convenient
to keep a tally of his sheep with marks on the ground or notches
on a stick, and eventually may have begun to group the tallies
into fives and tens (or hands, thumbs, and feet, if you like).
But still, two hands, a foot, and a few extra hands are not a
convenient way of handling even a number of that size. From
this dilemma emerged, eventually, the idea of having the value of
a number-word be represented by a particular symbol, and, ulti-
mately, the idea that the position of a symbol in an arrangement
of such number-symbols would determine its value.

The evidence is that such developments took place in
China as early as the twelfth century B.C., before the beginning
of the Christian era, and a little later in Mesopotamia. The
Chinese, who had an elaborate written language of pictographs,
worked out a positional number system (scale of notation, in
modern parlance) based on ten. The Sumerians, in Mesopotamia, used a base-sixty scale of notation—for what reason scholars are still debating (though base sixty still survives in the
division of hours or minutes into sixty). In both of these in-
stances, the pattern of development can only be guessed—full
development must have taken centuries—but it is not hard to
make a reasonable guess at the steps.

Suppose, for example, that the members of the New
Guinea tribe mentioned previously were able to develop their
number system from the present spoken "fingers," "hands,"
"thumbs" stage to a positional scale; they might well eventually
arrive at the Western system of a decimal scale.

There is another New Guinea tribe, which has a number
system based on "two." Their counting goes something like
this:

1   *urapun*
2   *okosa*
3   *okosa-urapun*
4   *okosa-okosa*
5   *okosa-okosa-urapun*
6   *okosa-okosa-okosa*

and over six, "many." Which is not too surprising, since twenty, for example, would be *okosa-okosa-okosa-okosa-okosa-okosa-okosa-okosa-okosa-okosa*. This could be a great motivation for the invention of multiplication.

On the other hand, digital computers, which are neither bored nor confused by repetition, operate quite efficiently in a base two scale. The computer does not find "llllll" a tongue-twisting way of saying "sixty-three."

In talking about this early development of number systems as bases for subsequent mathematics, we must stress rationality and usefulness—that which makes sense in terms of the needs of primitive people. There is another side to the primitive perception of number—that which may be called "number mysticism."

The first few pages of the Book of Genesis, for example, contain many references to the number seven. "And God blessed the seventh day, and sanctified it." Later there were seven good years and seven famine years associated with the story of Joseph in Egypt. Joshua and his men marched seven times around the walls of Jericho. Seven cords bound Samson, and Job offered up seven burnt offerings. Jesus talked of the seventy times seven forgivenesses. There are the seven seals of Revelation. The number seven had a special significance in the number mysticism of the Pythagoreans, which was revived again and again throughout the history of the West.

There are other numbers that have special, nonutilitarian significance. Among the Dogon of West Africa, for example, eight seems to mean completeness or wholeness. The body is believed to have eight joints, and the Dogon represent it with colored stones.

This image of the body apparently reflects the image they have of their society, for the lines between the joints give a model of the ideal social system. The first-ranked family in the Dogon myth marries with the eighth-ranked family; the second with the seventh, and so on. The marriages are arranged so that the sum of the ranks of the families (1+8, 2+7, 3+6, 4+5) is always 9, the number associated with the Dogon chieftainship.

In most parts of Africa, odd numbers—numbers that in one East African tribe are called those "without a companion"—are looked upon unfavorably. The Kikuyu of Kenya consider seven so unlucky that they even avoid the word for it as much as possible. Among the Tonga of South Africa, a group of people can be cursed if it is odd in number. They asked a visiting anthropologist why he wished to count them, thinking he wanted one of them to perish. Yet, how different are they from the American hostess who will not have thirteen at a dinner party?

In both the Indo-European area and the Americas, four is important because it is the number of the directions, it is the way the world is seen. Why, though, should the directions be thought of as "four," rather than, say "six"? A hypothesis involves a geometric visualization of numbers. Given an assortment of pebbles, a person, particularly an unsophisticated person, will arrange them in the shape of a square. Four pebbles are the smallest number with which you can form a square.

For whatever the reason, square numbers have had a ritual importance in various cultures, as have those numbers which are one more than a square—for the center of a square gives a feeling of position within the center of the cosmos.

For the Zuñi Indians, space is divided into six directions—

north, east, south, west, above, and below—but four, the number of the primary directions, is absolutely fundamental. In the beginning, the Zuñi ancestors lived in four underground "wombs," or levels, from which they were delivered by an emissary of the sun. The ancestors then wandered around for a long time, settling for four years and then moving on for four years, alternately—in search of the "middle place," the center of the world. Everything is done in fours in Zuñi: confinement lasts four days after a birth; the spirit is exorcised after a man's death with a stick waved four times around the head; the fourth time a question is asked of a man he must answer truthfully.

The Zuñi have a ritual calendar of amazing complexity. The year begins at the winter solstice and proceeds in random twenty-day periods to the summer solstice. A dance, in which the gods are impersonated, may be announced eight days ahead of time, be prepared for by eight days of abstinence, and last four days. The most sacred priest keeps track of these twenty-day periods, and on the basis of them the Zuñi regulate their desert agriculture. But they have no concern for the number of days in a year, nor in the number of years that pass—two matters that in many cultures have motivated the development of considerable mathematics. Numbers are important to the Zuñi, but not in any technical sense. The time sense of these people, and others who live agricultural lives, is cyclic, rather than linear, as we tend to view it. The year begins when the sun rises over a certain mountain, or, as it used to be with a tribe in the Philippines, when the young of a certain bird first said, "*Ki-ki.*" And this is the way time probably was regarded by the remote ancestors of those people who eventually evolved carefully calculated calendars—the Mayans, the Mesopotamians, the Incas.

But, as their way of life became more complicated, a more exact calendar was needed. This brought developments in mathematics, far beyond the simple counting processes that served the agricultural people well. And, as people turned from strictly agricultural activities to those of trade and business, they needed techniques for convenient calculation. There is yet another side to the development of mathematics—that of relating events in the lives of individuals to the relative positions of the stars and planets. (The astrologer continued to be important in even the more complicated cultures well into the "Western era," and for a long time "astrologer" was thought of as synonymous with "mathematician.")

2

THE WESTWARD MOVEMENT

The development of mathematics as we know it is usually traced to the people of Egypt and Mesopotamia (with some debt possibly owed to the Indian mathematicians) whose ideas eventually spread to Europe, there to form a basis for the substantial developments that began in the twelfth century A.D.

Apart from the Babylonian-Egyptian-Greek tradition, there were other mathematical developments. These sources—the Inca of Peru, the Maya of Central America, and the Chinese—contributed nothing to the European mathematical tradition, which is what we in this country follow (though there may have been more of an influence by the Chinese on Indian mathematics than has been suspected). But these cultures had much in common with those more in our "mainstream"—the problems of organizing and managing large-scale societies, and of providing satisfactory ideologies for them. These problems, in all the cultures, motivated the development of some kind of mathematical tradition—from the primitive accounting of the Inca Empire to the sophisticated astronomical mathematics of Mesopotamia.

As the Americas are not thought to have been inhabited by man until about fifteen or twenty thousand years ago, society developed later here than it did in the "old" countries of Asia and Europe. The agricultural revolution (when men learned to cultivate plants for food, and consequently could set up fixed communities) was consequently slower to develop. This change-over from nomadic, wandering life to one of stability was as drastic in its way as the industrial revolutions of the past 150 years have been for our own society. A highly developed society—which includes mathematics among its accomplishments —cannot exist without a food surplus. For it is made up of various kinds of people who are unproductive so far as food-gathering is concerned—priests, rulers, scribes, and soldiers, to name a few categories. Hunting and gathering produce barely enough food for everyone engaged in it—it is a full-time business for the whole of a society. Agriculture can be much more efficient.

Archaeologists are still uncertain about when and where maize was first cultivated by people in the Americas, but evidence points to Mexico, about 2500 B.C. This was a good four thousand years later than the cultivation of wheat and barley in the Near East. Over a period of one or two millennia, farming techniques became more efficient, and maize agriculture spread south to the Andean area.

Common art motifs, from the period between 800 to 300 B.C., indicate that there may have been direct contact between Mexico and Peru. In the first millennium of the Christian era, elaborate cultures developed along the Peruvian coast. The most impressive was that of the Mochica, which, around 1000 A.D., was consolidated into the Chimu Empire. The Chimu had no written language, so little is known about them except from archaeology. They irrigated the desert of coastal Peru by digging canals from the mountains (one was about seventy miles long and brought fresh water to sea level from a height of about 4,000 feet). They built elaborate cities or ceremonial centers, and step pyramids. The Chimu Empire was a conquest state based on military provinces. Its inhabitants worshiped the sun and the moon.

The precise layout of Chan Chan, their center, and the canal engineering indicate that the Chimu knew something of practical geometry, at the very least. (In this sense, they were like the Egyptians. And, there are some obvious similarities in the two cultures which have prompted people to suggest contact between them. Possibilities are presently being investigated.) But, when you come right down to it, we simply have no way of knowing anything about the mathematics of the Chimu, nor about any other aspect of their intellectual life.

Another early civilization of the Peruvian highland region was the Tiahuanaco Empire, which is even more enigmatic than the Chimu. The Tiahuanaco went on a march of conquest around 900 A.D., leaving their religious motif, the weeping god, all over the Andean area. They also left a circular golden disk, with a series of motifs carved around the rim. The design is symmetric and looks something like the Aztec calendar stone. It may be a calendar (which would suggest some mathematical accomplishment), or it may be a beautiful representation of a religious world view. Again, absence of writing has left present-day scholars in a position of merely guessing.

The empire of the Inca, another highland people, spread from an area around Cuzco to embrace most of Peru and parts of what are now Ecuador and Chile. The expansion began about 1438 A.D., and the empire was still being consolidated when a small group of Spanish conquistadors, under Francisco Pizarro, conquered it by killing the Supreme Inca, in 1527. The rapid conquest of highland and coastal Peru by the Inca (the Chimu gave them the hardest fight but fell in 1466) was a result of their effective military organization and their intelligent conquest policy: a conquered people was treated humanely and allowed insofar as possible to keep their old customs and gods, though the local gods were subordinated to the sun god of the Inca.

A few other conquering peoples have made a point of permitting their new subjects to continue their old ways—religious forms, in particular. The Moslems, for example, tolerated Christianity and Judaism for many years, to their own considerable advantage. The Mongols, while hardly "humane" in some of their policies, did encourage Moslem and Nestorian Christian scholars within their empire—again to their own advantage.

The Inca had no written mathematical notation or written language. They managed their vast empire, more than two thousand miles long, through *quipus*—knotted ropes based on a positional decimal number system. A quipu consisted of a main cord to which were tied a number of smaller knotted strands. On one of the smaller strands, a single knot in the row farthest from the main cord represented one. A knot in the next farthest row represented ten; in one row closer, one hundred, and so on.

If a strand had no knot in a certain row (as in cord B in the hundreds, and cord C in the tens), there were no units of that order. That is, the Inca used an implicit zero, though it was probably not thought of in such an abstract way by the Inca. The "zero" was simply a blank space where most of the other cords on the quipu had knots. The "empty column" type of zero worked better for the Inca than it did for people in other areas who had a written language and written mathematical notation. For these, the empty column caused confusion, since the blank was not always so obvious as it was in the quipus.

Quipus carried more information than just numbers. The color of the strings, for example, might tell the character of the numerical facts. Yellow could mean "gold" or "maize"; white could mean "silver" or, more abstractly, "peace"; and red could mean "war." Also, there was a certain unalterable order to the way people and things were arranged. From the main cord of a quipu for population, the first set of strands represented men, the second set, women, and the third set, children. Weapons were ordered: spears, arrows, bows, javelins, clubs, axes, and slings.

The quipus also served, in the absence of written records, as mnemonic devices for oral tradition. A few *amantas*—wise men—were chosen in each reign to compose stories and songs about the current Inca's career—of his defeats as well as his victories—and somehow to encode them on quipus. The quipus and the history were then passed on together to the next generation of amantas.

These historical quipus were not like written records, however, for their configurations simply reminded the amantas of stories they had been told by elders. Thus, there is not much hope that quipus found in archaeological excavations today can be "cracked," as the cuneiform tablets of Mesopotamia have been. They are only so many knotted strings.

What will some archaeologist of some future date think about the quipus used by the United States Navy to show distances between ships that are transferring supplies and fuel? They also are in color—the colored bands are ten feet apart—and there is a mnemonic that goes with them—"Rub your back with grease," for red, yellow, black, white, green.

The Inca Empire was not only administered through the decimal system of the quipus; it was actually structured according to base ten. The Supreme Inca topped a single, all-encompassing hierarchy. Under him, in decreasing order of rank, was a pyramid of officials:

1. *Apu-cuna*—four officials (viceroys) each in charge of one of four quarters of the empire.
2. *Tucuiricuc-cuna*—governors of the provinces, each of 40,000 households.
3. *Hunu-camaya-cuna*—officials in charge of 10,000 households.
4. *Huaranca-camayu-cuna*—officials in charge of 1,000 households.
5. *Pichca-pachaca-camayu-cuna*—who governed 500 households.

This illustration, showing a Peruvian quipu, related to a counting board, in the lower left, was drawn by a Peruvian Indian, D. Felipe Poma de Ayala, sometime between 1583 and 1613. It and other pen-and-ink sketches accompanied his manuscript and, when finally rediscovered, were of great help in resolving the problem of how the Inca performed his calculations. Courtesy Scripta Mathematica.

6. *Pachaca-camayu-cuna*—leaders of 100 households.
7. *Pichca-chunca-camayu-cuna*—with 50 households each to look after.
8. *Chunca-camayu-cuna*—who kept an eye on 10 households.

Very little is known about the particulars of the religious ideology of the Inca, but apparently they, like most American people, held the number four sacred. In the beginning, accord-

	A	B	C	D	
10000	O O 5×10000 O O O	O 3×50000 O O O	O 2 × 150000 O	O 300000	a
1000	O O 5× 1000 O O O	O 3 × 5000 O O O	O 2 × 15000 O	O 30000	b
100	O O 5 × 100 O O O	O 3 × 500 O O O	O 2 × 1500 O	O 3000	c
10	O O 5 × 10 O O O	O 3 × 50 O O O	O 2 × 150 O	O 300	d
1	O O 5 × 1 O O O	O 3 × 5 O O O	O 2 × 15 O	O 30	e
	1	5	15	30	

This schematic represents an attempt to interpret a "counting board." The counting board is related to the quipu, which was used for record keeping on numerical data. Note the apparent combination of bases for the number system of the Inca.

ing to their myth, four brothers and four sisters set out to find a place to live, and one survived to found the city of Cuzco. Deference to the number four is reflected in the fact that there were four quarters of the kingdom, and 40,000 households in each province. Otherwise, the administrative hierarchy was based strictly on ten and seemed to be designed to simplify, as much as possible, the "bookkeeping" of managing the empire.

That is, if every unit of the hierarchy contained either five or ten of the units of the next lower level, no complicated multiplication or division was necessary to calculate, say, how many bushels of grain the five of a level-eight division must each produce in order to fulfill a pichca-chunca-camayu-cuna's taxation quota of 100 bushels.

The system worked well enough, even as an approximation to the ideal. There was no need for 100 per cent efficiency among a people with as simple a way of life as was that of the Inca, even those of the royal class. The very existence of this mathematically simple ideal structure indicates that Incan mathematics itself was rudimentary—involving, most likely, only addition and subtraction.

Although one might suppose it to have been easy enough to lay the quipus alongside each other and perform addition and subtraction directly, according to the early Spanish chroniclers, calculations were performed with counting boards and small stones. Here, again, there is an analogue in the Roman tradition. Roman numerals were used for the purpose of conveying information, but calculations were performed on counting boards.

The accounting for the Inca Empire was done by a class of quipu scribes who handed down their techniques from father to son. There were such scribes at each level of the administrative hierarchy, and, beginning at the provincial level, a scribe specialized in a single category of quipu—for population, for military supplies, for foodstuffs, and so on.

These scribes were expected to have well-trained memories and, presumably, be able to do some mental arithmetic. Death was the penalty for forgetfulness or inaccuracy. The scribes were dependent, as was everyone else, on the Supreme Inca. They were in no sense an independent intellectual class—though they were something of an elite group—for knowing the quipus was the secret that made the empire possible.

"Science," one Inca sage is supposed to have observed, "was not intended for the people, but for those of generous blood. Persons of low degree are only puffed up by it, and rendered vain and arrogant." A later Inca expressed the aphorism "He who attempts to count the stars, not even knowing how to count the knots of the quipus, ought to be held in derision."

Besides the royal class of the Inca, an official and scribal bureaucracy and a nobility drawn partly from the ruling classes of conquered peoples, the rank and file supported a priesthood that maintained the temples of the sun. These temple priests were probably responsible for keeping the calendar, which was not complex. The year consisted of twelve months and began on June 21, the winter solstice in the Southern Hemisphere. Observations of the solstices and the equinoxes allowed the priests to make up for the approximately eleven-day discrepancy between the lunar and solar year by adding six extra days throughout the year, and a five-day period at the end. According to a Spanish chronicler, a rectangular arrangement of eight towers outside Cuzco was used to determine the solstices. The equinoxes were fixed by a gnomon or pillar device, which may have been located at Quito, almost on the equator.

So, with a very minimum of "bookkeeping mathematics," a simple calendar, a government structure that subordinated people to a decimal ordering and placed everyone in a strict hierarchy under the Supreme Inca, the empire of the Inca survived and probably would have flourished had not Pizarro and his followers happened along. The system continued to function for years after the coming of the conquistadors, and most Spanish commentators admit that the people were far better off under the Incas than under the Spanish.

The culture of the Maya, in the Yucatán jungle, several thousand miles to the north of the realm of the Inca, provides a sharp contrast with the culture of the Inca. The Maya, incidentally, flourished long before the empire of the Inca—a general collapse came about 900 A.D., though certain enclaves survived in the north until the Spanish conquest. The extent of Mayan civilization was not suspected at all until the jungle-covered cities were discovered in the 1840s.

The Maya had a sophisticated written language that combined ideographs (some symbols represented ideas, as in Chinese writing) and phonographs (other symbols represented sounds, as in our own alphabetic system). Of the language, in general, very little is known. The Spanish had a chance to learn about it from remnants of the Mayan people at the time of their invasion, but they were not interested. Number-glyphs and calendar-glyphs though, have been fairly easy to interpret.

Actually, the Maya had two ways of representing numbers. The simpler was a bar-and-dot scheme, with three basic symbols. They combined the dots and bars to form numerals up to 9—which, of course, were necessary in a base-twenty system. And, they used these "digits" to form numerals in a positional notation, from top to bottom. Where, for example, in our decimal scale, we would mean by 24,372:

2 times ten^4+4 times ten^3+3 times ten^2+7 times ten^1+2 times ten^0, the Maya would represent the same number as:

three times twenty^3 (which we call 24,000)
zero times twenty^2 (still zero, however you count it)
eighteen times twenty
twelve times twenty^0

This number system was quite an amazing achievement, particularly impressive when you realize that our own system, complete with zero, did not become really operational until the thirteenth century, at the earliest, and it was a long time after that before Europeans reluctantly gave up their counting boards.

Earliest monumental use of this positional base-twenty system appears to correspond to December 9, 36 B.C.

No examples of arithmetic calculations have been found, and possibly the Mayan priests, who were the principal users of mathematics, did all the work mentally. The essential addition and multiplication tables were very simple. More than that, cacao merchants had bar-and-dot counters (forerunners of the cuisenaire rods, no doubt, and not unlike Chinese rod-numerals) with which they calculated on flat surfaces.

Mathematics was very important to the priests' calendar calculations, which were the basis of Mayan ideology and religion. The Maya—at least the priests—observed two calendars. They had a sacred year that was generated by the meshing, as in gears, of two cycles—the sacred numbers 1 through 13, and the twenty named days.

As the cycles turn like gears, the sacred-year names are generated: 1 Ik, 2 Akbal, 3 Ken, 13 Ix, 1 Men, 2 Clb, and so on. They will come back to the position 1 Ik after 260 days, when the sacred year is completed. A man's birthday in the sacred year determined his fate for life as in Western astrology, and the god of the named day was his patron and protector.

The vague year had eighteen twenty-day months and one five-day month at the end of the year, which was a period of celebration—imagine a five-day New Year's celebration! And, the Maya designated any one day by its names in both calendars. This produced a double count of days for the sacred and vague years, and has been called the "calendar round." Again, you may find it convenient to think of it in terms of the meshing of two gears.

The calendar round—during which no day name was repeated—lasted the period of days that is the least common multiple of 260 and 365—18,980 days, or 73 sacred years and 52 vague years.

The calendar round is an especially beautiful and systematic expression of a cyclic concept of time, and was shared by peoples all over Central America. The Maya apparently had a mythology that described three worlds before the present one, each destroyed by flood. Mayan Indians today believe that the present "world" is the fourth and, like the first three, will end in flood.

The Aztec, who lived in the area we now call Mexico, also subscribed to the calendar round view of time and expected the world to end at the end of the calendar round. On the last night of the round, the population of the Aztec capital gathered on the hills of Mexico City and waited anxiously for the dawn. The rising sun was met with rejoicing, for it meant another fifty-two years of life.

The Maya had an even lengthier cycle than the calendar round. This was called "long count." Long count was built up

> 20 kins or days=1 uinal
> 18 uinals=1 tun (365 days)
> 20 tuns=1 katun (7,200 days)
> 20 katuns=1 batkun (144,000 days)

from and the Great Cycle consisted of 13 batkuns, a period of just about 5,125 years. They deviated from the base-twenty scheme by throwing in the 18 uinals=1 tun.

The oldest dated Mayan monument, that which mentions a date corresponding to our December 9, 36 B.C., indicates that it was inscribed "7 batkuns, 16 katuns, 3 tuns, 2 uinals, and 13 kins" since the beginning of the era. That would place it about 3113 B.C., at which time, archaeological evidence indicates, the inhabitants of Central America were still hunters and gatherers. So, the date must have been a mythological one for the beginning of the present world—one adopted much later.

This Great Cycle meant, for the Maya, that the world was not likely to run out at the end of every calendar round. The present Great Cycle, and the present world, could not end until December 24, 2011.

The Maya made still one more combination of cycles. Any date was designated on a monument not only by its long-count name, but also by its position in the calendar round. For example, one monument reads: 9117.0.0.0 (long count), 13 Ahau (sacred year), 18 Cumhu (vague year), a designation that would not come up again for some 374,440 years. Which means that, for practical purposes, the Mayan priests had a system in which every date is unique, but they still had not abandoned, in theory anyway, the cyclic view of time which was so important in their religion.

The Mayan time-reckoning is a totally abstract system. Even the vague year was exactly 365 days, while the true year is more accurately given as 365.2422 days. I suspect most Maya were not troubled by this, just as most people of our time would not really be concerned if the year were adjusted to some regular length, rather than having that 366-day year thrown in, or having no leap year at certain century marks. But the priests were very much aware of the true year, and they worked out its length to amazing accuracy. The priests of Copán, in the sixth or seventh century, developed a formula for intercalation based on a true year of 365.2420 days. This is closer than our Gregorian year of 365.2425 days, adopted in 1582.

The Maya also knew the synodic year of Venus (the period it took the planet to return to a certain point on the horizon). They figured 584 days, which is not far off from the value usually given these days of 583.92 days. They also noted an eight-year cycle: five Venus "years"=8 vague years ($5 \times 584 = 8 \times 365$). One of their books that survived appears to have a multiplication table for 78, indicating that perhaps the priests knew the synodic year of Mars, 780 days. Another book has a list of lunar periods when eclipses of the sun or moon are most likely.

The number four was important because it indicated the directions, and their underworld consisted of nine levels (going Dante two better—but then Dante was caught up with the mystic seven of Western tradition). The sum of the four and nine gives the thirteen that was quite important in their calendar cycles—and, I suppose, you could point out that these are really the first two square numbers.

I'll leave the speculation to you, and turn to Chinese "mathematics in a social context"—for which there is much more evidence.

3

AND IN THE FAR EAST

Both Pythagoras and Thales are reported to have traveled in Egypt and Mesopotamia picking up mathematical lore as they went, and bringing it back to Greece. There is no report that either of these scholars reached China. And this is unfortunate, since they could have brought back the idea of a positional, base-ten number system, which could have made a remarkable difference in the development of Greek mathematics.

Still, the history of Chinese mathematics has only recently been given serious consideration in the West. There was, in fact, contact between the Greek and Roman world and China at a very early date, but there seems to be little evidence to suggest the exchange of mathematical ideas, among other intellectual matters. Apparently, the two mathematical worlds developed independently, though there are some similarities.

From the period of the Han dynasty of 200 B.C. to the revolution of 1911, China was a single society, organized on a single set of social principles. The principles were those of Confucianism, a rational, pragmatic philosophy, which taught a single universal law, *tao*, governing the actions of the universe and of man. Chinese philosophy was aware of the "problem of order," which Western philosophy rediscovered in the seventeenth century. But, while the West was concerned with social order, the Chinese tried to understand the order of the universe, in which man played a small part.

One Chinese metaphor for order—one model for the tao—was mathematics. According to Chinese legend, the mythical hero who invented the state also created mathematics: "Dragon-bodied Fu-Hsi first established kingly rule, drew the eight triangles, devised the knotted cords, in order to govern all within the four seas." Since Chinese society was the most carefully and consistently rational of the cultures existing at that time, it seems appropriate that it should have seen its own social order as closely associated wtih the mathematical.

The earliest historical state in China was the Shang, which built walled cities in the north Chinese river valleys in the middle of the second millennium B.C. The Shang worked out the earliest writing in China, a pictographic system that grew into the elaborate ideographic writing of classical China. The Shang priests wrote questions to the gods in their script on oracle bones, heated the bones until they cracked, and interpreted the gods' answers according to the cracks. The written symbol on an oracle bone was often a close portrayal of what it referred to. Thus the sun was represented as a circle with a dot in it, and the moon as a sort of crescent. But there remained ideas which could not be drawn directly; even in the Shang, ideographs had to be devised. So "brightness" was represented by combining the pictographs for the sun and the moon. The abstraction "virtue" took more ingenuity. It was represented with the left half of the pictograph for crossroads, which connoted "the right way of doing things," and the pictographs for the eye and the heart. These pictographs became stylized and abstract by the time of the Han dynasty, but Chinese writing has remained ideographic (rather than phonetic), requiring today more than 7,000 symbols for its vocabulary.

A literate culture obviously can become far more elaborate than an illiterate culture. A sage no longer has to know all his teachers personally. By the fourth century B.C., Chinese philosophers had developed a sophisticated world view based on two forces and five elements. The forces were "yang" and "yin," male and female, active and passive forces pervading the universe and found in all things. The elements were water, fire, wood, metal, and earth, not thought of as specific substances, but more as examples of physical states:

Water	soaking, dripping, descending	liquidity, fluidity, solution	saltiness
Fire	heating, burning, ascending	heat, combustion	bitterness
Wood	accepting form by submitting to cutting and carving instruments	solidity involving workability	sourness
Metal	accepting form by molding in a liquid state, and capable of remolding	solidity involving moldability	acridity
Earth	producing edible vegetation	nutritiveness	sweetness

The Chinese fitted hundreds of different things into this five-fold classification. For instance:

	seasons	directions	numbers	musical notes	animals	emotions	planets
Wood	spring	east	8	chio	scaly (fishes)	anger	Jupiter
Fire	summer	south	7	shih	feathered (birds)	joy	Mars
Earth	(sixth month)	center	5	kung	naked (man)	desire	Saturn
Metal	autumn	west	9	shang	hairy (mammals)	sorrow	Venus
Water	winter	north	6	yu	shell-covered	fear	Mercury

Five was so important for its connotation of order that the Han dynasty used it on its emblem. The five elements even gave the Chinese philosophers a way of explaining the rise and fall of ruling houses for the empire. An emperor, they postulated,

Development of mathematics seems to have gone hand in hand with development and application of religion in most cultures. The priests had the time to work out the mathematics, learning to know which questions to ask, and finding the need for some systematic methods for predicting behavior of celestial phenomena.

ruled only by virtue of one of the five elements. So as wood overcomes earth, as metal overcomes wood, as fire overcomes metal, as water overcomes fire, and as earth overcomes water, so there is a cyclical rise and fall of dynasties.

Things that did not fit into the fivefold classification were put into orders of 4s, or 9s, or 28s. A mirror of the T'ang dynasty (618–906 A.D.), which promises wisdom to anyone who looks into it, has in concentric circles the 28 mansions of the heavens, the 8 trigrams of the Book of Changes, the 12 animals of the animal cycle, and the 4 animals of the celestial palaces. An example of mystical numbers, of the way numbers can give meaning to the world, is a text of the third century B.C. The text begins: "The principle of Change has brought into existence men, birds, animals, and all varieties of creeping things." And it continues with this demonstration:

Heaven is 1, earth is 2, man is 3. 3 times 3 makes 9. 9 times 9 makes 81. 1 governs the sun. The sun's number is 10. Therefore man is born in the tenth month.

8 times 9 makes 72, an even number after an odd. Odd numbers govern time, time governs the moon. The moon governs the horse. Therefore the horse has a gestation period of 11 months.

7 times 9 makes 63. 3 governs the Great Bear (Great Dipper). This constellation governs the dog. Therefore the dog is born after 3 months.

6 times 9 makes 54. 4 governs the seasons. Seasons govern the pig. Therefore the pig has a gestation period of 4 months.

5 times 9 makes 45. 5 governs musical notes. The notes govern the monkey. Therefore the monkey is born after 5 months.

4 times 9 makes 36. 6 governs the pitch pipes. The pitch pipes govern the deer. Therefore the deer is 6 months in the womb.

3 times 9 makes 27. 7 governs the stars. The stars govern the tiger. Therefore the tiger's gestation is 7 months.

9 times 9 makes 81. 8 governs the wind, the wind governs insects. Therefore insects change in the eighth month.

In another era, I suspect, one might have written off such statements as "nonsense" or, at best, "quaint." But, at a time when learned men spend much time and money investigating "particles" which have no mass, no position and for whose duration new, small numbers had to be invented, it may be easier to interpret this "number mysticism" in another way—as an attempt by primitive people to develop a universal law, or explanation for their universe. Today, scientists are trying to do the same thing—on the basis of particles and electromagnetic waves.

China had been conquered about 1122 B.C. by a people who established the Chou dynasty. The Chou had a cult of heaven, worshiping the sun and the stars, but it was without priests. So the old Shang priesthood became a class of scribes in the service of the Chou rulers. In the period of disintegration and warfare that followed, the "period of the Warring States," the scribes became more important as scholars, wandering among the feudal courts and providing each ruler with the genealogical proof that he was descending from the Son of Heaven—i.e., was fit to be emperor of all China. It was a period of intellectual ferment, a time when most of the important philosophical traditions of China emerged.

During the period of the Warring States, there was a school of philosophers in China, the Mohists, who were interested in the sort of abstract mathematical ideas that proved so fundamental to pure mathematics in Greece. The Mohists defined the point, for example:

> The line is divided into parts and that part which has no remaining part (i.e., cannot be divided into still smaller parts and thus forms the extreme end of a line) is a point.

They also struggled with the difficult ideas of infinitesimals, the root of Zeno's paradoxes in the West:

> If you keep on cutting a line into half, you will come to a state in which there is "almost nothing," and since nothing cannot be halved, this can no more be cut.

But this generalizing tradition in Chinese mathematics did not flourish for complex political and social reasons. The

There is a certain gracefulness to the early Chinese architecture, which you might compare with the Greeks. No one that I know of has yet suggested the Chinese applied the subtle mathematical methods to produce this gracefulness, as did the Greeks, in their architecture.

centralization that brought the period of the Warring States to a close was supported philosophically by the legalists, a school of thought which might even be called antiphilosophical. For the Mohists had a philosophical doctrine that emphasized universal love, while the Confucians and Taoists based their philosophies on two different interpretations of the tao—the first as universal order, the second as mystical truth—the legalists said all philosophical speculation was meaningless and fruitless. What China needed was law and authority. The harsh Ch'in dynasty, which unified China by conquest, put the legalists' philosophy into practice. At one point, the Ch'in emperor, in order to centralize knowledge and destroy the influence of the wandering scholars, ordered the burning of all the books in China, except for a select few extolling the Ch'in.

Within twenty-five years, there was a reaction to the brutality of the Ch'in, but the dynasty had accomplished its purpose. China was centralized, with an official bureaucracy and the scholars subordinated to state authority. Confucianism was a more humane philosophy than legalism, but it did not encourage abstract thinking in mathematics.

The unification meant more than all China's subordination to one supreme ruler. Weights and measures were standardized. While the old lineal measures had been based on parts of the body, the new measures were based on powers of ten.

The old system of measures made calculation difficult because of its uneven nature.

(8 fingers)	8 tshun=1 chih	(1 woman's hand)
(10 fingers)	10 tshun=1 chih	(1 man's hand)
(8 woman's hands)	8 chih =1 hsun	(1 forearm)
	2 hsun =1 chang	
	16 chih =1 chang	

Which is almost as strange a system as one in which

12 inches=1 foot (average of men leaving church)
3 feet   =1 yard (tip of nose to tip of finger)
5½ yards =1 rod

and so on.

Axle widths on carts were standardized, for the roads of China were worn in ruts the width of a cart's axle. Administration of the country was rationalized into a series of bureaucratic levels starting at the provinces and progressing through districts to the court at Peking with its nine royal advisers. A monumental barrier was built along the northern border to keep out the barbarians. The Great Wall of China, according to legend, was constructed at the cost of a million lives.

Chinese mathematics had a powerful tool in its positional base-ten number system. In its earliest appearance on the oracle bones, the Chinese decimal system was more advanced than contemporary Babylonian and Egyptian numbers. By the second century B.C., the number system had grown into a simple and rational one, with a written form that shows the influence of counting rods.

The system's two sets of digits, one vertical and the other horizontal, meant that a specific symbol for zero was not really necessary. In our own horizontal system, confusion would result if we adopted the solution of, say, the Inca to the "problem of zero," by leaving a blank. 4 7 2 (40702) could be misinterpreted as 4702 or as 472. In Chinese notation, however, 40702 would be written with the vertical set of symbols only. The absence of horizontal numerals between the symbols implies the two blanks, so there is no confusion.

The Chinese probably acquired the zero from the Indians, though, indeed, the relationship between Chinese and Indian mathematics is still being debated. The zero has been found in inscriptions dating to about 875 in India and earlier in Indo-China. Earlier, Indian mathematicians had discussed the properties of the number. By contrast, the Babylonians used a zero at least as early as 300 B.C.

Chinese mathematics shows a strong arithmetic-algebraic flavor, contrasted to the geometric form that characterizes Greek mathematics. The Greeks, of course, did not have the convenient number system and notation that the Chinese used.

The earliest Chinese mathematics books show the transition from the "number mysticism" to practical applications. While the dating of these books is debatable, the oldest apparently was one whose title is usually translated *The Arithmetical Classic of the Gnomon and the Circular Paths of the Heavens*. (You will often see it referred to by the first two words of the Chinese, transliterated as *Chou Pei.*)

Much of the *Chou Pei* is written as a dialogue between Chou King, a ruler of one province, and Shang Kao, who evidently was a scholar:

"Of old, Chou King addressed Shang Kao, saying, 'I have heard that the Grand Prefect [Shang Kao] is versed in the art of numbering. May I venture to inquire how Fu-Hsi anciently established the degrees of the celestial sphere? There are no steps by which one may ascend the heavens, and the earth is not measurable with a foot-rule. I should like to ask you what was the origin of those numbers?'

"Shang Kao replied, 'The art of numbering proceeds from the circle and the square. The circle is derived from the square and the square from the rectangle.' "

(It is interesting to note that "rectangle" was interpreted literally as "T-square" or "carpenter's square"—suggesting a practical consideration at one time or another.) Anyway, the dialogue goes on to describe the relationship between the sides of the 3, 4, 5 right triangle—a business that Shang Kao called "piling up the rectangles."

Shang Kao goes on to bring in the name of Yu the Great, the patron saint of hydraulic engineers, whose "methods for governing the world were derived from these right triangle numbers."

"Chou King exclaimed, 'Great indeed is the art of numbering. I would like to ask about the Tao of the use of the right-angled triangle.'

"Shang Kao replied, 'The plane right-angled triangle serves to lay out straight and square cords. The recumbent right-angled triangle serves to observe heights. The reversed right-angled triangle serves to fathom depths. The flat right-angled triangle is used for ascertaining distances. By the revolution of a right-angled triangle a circle is formed. By uniting right-angled triangles squares are formed. The square pertains to earth, the circle belongs to heavens.

" 'He who understands the earth is a wise man, and he who understands the heavens is a sage. Knowledge is derived from the straight line. The straight line is derived from the right angle. And the combination of the right angle with numbers is what guides and rules the ten thousand things.'

"Chou King exclaimed, 'Excellent indeed!'"

When you come right down to it, Shang Kao was quite right—you can get a great deal of mileage out of the right triangle.

The *Arithmetical Rules in Nine Sections* (or chapters) is another frequently cited Chinese mathematical classic. It was compiled, apparently, from fragments of the ancient texts that had survived the book burning by Chang Tsang, who had survived the burning of scholars along with books. Actually, Chang Tsang earned a reputation first as a soldier under the first Han emperor. He turned to civil pursuits, rose to become the chief minister, and became a financial wizard.

The *Nine Sections* included 246 problems on such matters as the surveying of land (with abundant rules for computing areas and working with fractions) ; percentages and proportions; partnership situations; constructions—walls, dikes, canals, etc.; and taxation, as well as some that you may recognize now as puzzle types.

"Suppose there are a number of rabbits and pheasants confined in a cage, in all 35 heads and 94 feet. How many are there of each?"

Or how about this one, which later appeared in manuscripts in India and Europe: "What is the depth of a pond ten feet square if a reed growing in the center and extending one foot above the water just reaches the surface if drawn to the edge of the pool?"

Chang Tsang intended that this mathematics book should instruct, and included explanations of solutions, even getting involved in such matters as the division of fractions. Try this one:

"There is a [rectangular] field whose breadth is one pace and a half and a third. If the area is 1 pu [240 square paces], what will be the length of the field?"

He gives the answer as 130 10/11 paces.

Apart from the observation that the decimalization of the measurement units apparently did not carry over to the textbooks, the "rule" for the solution is intriguing—possibly because recent writers of mathematics textbooks have tried so hard to make division of fractions reasonable.

The Chinese used positive and negative numbers at an early date, and here is one of Chang Tsang's rules for using them:

"When equi-named [presumably same-signed] quantities are to be subtracted and the difference names are to be added, if the positive quantity has no opponent, make it negative; and if a negative has no opponent, make it positive. When the different named are to be subtracted, and the same-named are to be added, if a positive quantity has no opponent, make it positive, and if a negative has no opponent, make it negative."

Some 2,100 years later, writers of mathematics texts are proposing rules for adding and subtracting signed numbers.

The engineer-emperor Yu the Great is associated in Chinese legend with a magic square that is said to have shown up on the shell of a turtle, and another special array of numbers which was a gift of a dragon horse from the Yellow River.

This is, of course, the simplest magic square, with each row, column, and diagonal adding up to fifteen. The Chinese evidently were intrigued by it, as indeed were many Moslem writers, for there are references to magic squares, circles, and cubes throughout mathematical literature.

The Chinese developed several forms of digital calculations—and there are references to such systems in the classical Roman writers as well as such Anglo-Saxon commentators as the Venerable Bede. Both the ancient Chinese and the Romans played a number game with fingers, similar to that which Italians now call *morra*.

The abacus is usually associated with Eastern peoples, but it developed comparatively late in China, possibly because the ancient Chinese had other mechanical aids to calculation. At a very early date government officials used quipus, much like those used in the Inca Empire, and for the same purpose.

The quipus were not nearly so widely used as the counting rods. These date at least to the fourth or third centuries before the beginning of what is known in the West as the Christian era, and were originally simply sticks of bamboo or bone, of varying lengths, which could be bundled together. Much later, the counting rods were made of cast iron. Apparently calculations were made through the formation of rod numerals on a counting board—and again there is a parallel with the Romans, though the Romans used disks on their counting boards.

This may seem hardly an efficient method of calculation, but one astronomer, Wei Pho, is said to have "moved the counting-rods as if they were flying, so quickly that the eye could not follow their movements before the result was obtained."

Much earlier the philosopher Lao Tzu had noted that "Good mathematicians do not use counting rods." But apparently his puristic notion did not catch on, for it was common practice for government officials and engineers to carry their bags of counting rods at their girdles, much as the field engineer today carries his slide rule hanging from his belt.

Counting rods were eventually replaced by the abacus as a calculating device, but this was much later—after Europeans became influential in China.

The Chinese combined the applied methods of the Romans, in their architecture and fortifications, with theoretical mathematical developments that are only now being appreciated, largely through the efforts of Joseph Needham and his associates.

In addition to using mathematics in their engineering projects and in connection with problems of administering the government operations, the ancient Chinese applied mathematics to the business of devising a calendar and, to an extent, to astronomy.

Surprisingly, perhaps, the calendar-making was the more significant activity at the time, mathematically speaking, anyway. We have become rather used to establishing a calendar and living with it for hundreds of years, despite minor imperfections that could result in losing a day or so in some thousands of years. But apparently, the Chinese emperors of this period blamed natural and social disasters on the calendar. And, after such a setback of the orderly scheme of things, the emperor would order the mathematician to make him a new calendar.

Early Chinese astronomy involved little mathematics. It

was almost completely observational and as such has come off a poor second compared with the efforts of the people of the Mediterranean area. However, the Chinese did keep meticulous records, which are in fact the only consistent accounts of astronomical matters from the period extending from the fifth century B.C. to the tenth century A.D. And, if Chinese astronomy had no mathematical basis, it at least was not restricted by a mathematical bias. The following quotation from a Chinese astronomer reflects some of the ideas that were current:

"The sun, the moon, and the company of the stars float in the empty space, moving or standing still. All are condensed vapor. Thus the seven luminaries sometimes appear and sometimes disappear, sometimes move forward and sometimes retrograde, seeming to follow each a different series of regularities; their advances and recessions are not the same. It is because they are not rooted or tied together that their movements can vary so much. Among the heavenly bodies, the pole star always keeps its place, and the Great Bear never sinks below the horizon in the west as do the other stars. The seven luminaries [sun, moon, and five planets] all fall back westwards, the sun making one degree a day and the moon thirteen degrees. Their speed depends on their individual natures, which shows that they are not attached to anything, for if they were fastened to the body of heaven, this could not be so."

As Confucianism became the dominant social philosophy, gaining favor over the Taoists, orthodoxy was enforced in China. It was the Taoists who expounded the "infinite space" theory and were generally inclined toward scientific investigation. The Confucians gave theoretical and experimental science little heed, and this led to an eclipse of Chinese science and mathematics.

4

FROM THE LAND BETWEEN
THE TWO RIVERS

The people of Mesopotamia—"the land between the two rivers"
—took a somewhat more pessimistic view of nature than did,
say, the Chinese of the Middle Kingdom. This point of view
must reflect the greater uncertainties of the environment in that
part of the world, a point of view that seems justified when you
note that natural causes contributed significantly to the bury-
ing of the evidence of civilization in the area for many centuries.

So, while the Chinese could talk in terms of an orderly nature and social structure, begun by a mythological figure with
an inclination toward mathematics, the people of Mesopotamia
viewed the natural processes as unruly, and, hence, not to be
accounted for by mathematics. Here is one of their chants:

> Destructive storms and evil winds are they,
> An evil blast that heralds the bane-ful storm,
> An evil blast, forerunner of the bane-ful storm,
> They are the mighty children, mighty sons,
> Heralds of the Pestilence,
> Throne-bearers of Minkigal,
> They are the flood which rushes through the land.
>
> . . .
>
> Seven evil gods
> Seven evil demons,
> Seven evil demons of oppression,
> Seven in heaven and seven on earth.

They did find, though, that mathematics provided them with tools for controlling their environment.

Mesopotamia was "rediscovered" in the nineteenth century. Until then the Egyptians were credited with being the principal source of pre-Greek civilization in general and mathematics in particular. For unruly nature—shifts in the river system and changes in the climate—had changed the plain of the Tigris and Euphrates into a desert. The inhabitants were Arab nomads who wandered among the principal geological feature, the flat-topped hills, or tells.

In 1842, Paul Botta, a French official, dug into one of these tells and discovered an ancient Assyrian city, the capital of a ruler known as Sargon II. Since that time, archaeologists have excavated throughout the area and have deciphered the language, which was preserved through inscriptions on baked clay tablets, and we now have a picture of a civilization older, less tranquil, and apparently more important in Western development than that of Egypt.

A well-advanced culture flourished in Mesopotamia thousands of years before the time of the Greeks, but the Greek debt to the Mesopotamians, particularly in mathematics, has seldom been emphasized.

Study a map of Mesopotamia in its present state, and you will see how useless the sand is without artificial irrigation. On the other hand, the wealth and power of the ancient civilizations show what human planning can do with the rich alluvial plain between the rivers.

However, the process of civilizing the area began in the piedmont zone, north of Mesopotamia. There the agricultural revolution was underway by 6000 B.C., as man, in small villages such as Jarmo, domesticated wheat, barley, and animals. During the next few thousand years, the agriculturalists moved south into the plain; they built larger towns and irrigation canal systems, developed a religion that prompted them to erect some monumental architecture, and began to study the stars and planets and attribute to their movements an influence on the fates of men, individually and collectively. All of these activities motivated the invention of some mathematics.

The earliest culture in the area was that of the Sumerians, whose outlook was dominated by that pessimistic view of nature and, in particular, of man's position. The world was divided into two antithetical realms—heaven and earth. Heaven was the home of an elaborate assortment of gods who acted in an arbitrary and willful manner toward man. Both individually and collectively man was at the mercy of the gods and existed only to serve them. This indicates the need for temples, where such service could be organized and focused, and priests, who could organize the less enlightened and serve as intermediaries between the man-in-the-street and the gods. Each Sumerian city-state had its own patron-god, in whose name the land was owned. The priests administered this land. All the agricultural produce and some of the craft-goods were taken by the producers to the temple. A small portion was sacrificed by the priests to the patron-god; a larger portion was stored in the temple granary against famine, and the remainder was redistributed to the people.

The priests' important role in society came about gradually. Before the cities developed, political power in the villages had been held by councils of elders, and this tradition was continued in the city-states. In a time of crisis, the elders would elect a *lugal*—a "big man"—to lead the army. As the Mesopotamian plain became crowded with powerful cities, competing for land and for canal rights, politics became one long crisis. The lugal became a permanent political leader, and eventually his office became hereditary—much like a kingship. But at no time in Mesopotamian history did the lugal become divine in the sense of the Supreme Inca or the Pharaoh of Egypt. He was, like every other Sumerian, merely a servant of the gods.

That is, the Sumerians valued political authority less (though they recognized its practical necessity) and gave the priesthood more freedom and authority than did any of the other early civilizations, with the possible exception of the Mayan. Since, in any of the early civilizations, the priests were the thinkers, the keepers and interpreters of the traditions and the literate class, the status of the priesthood often had a great deal to do with how a cultural tradition, such as mathematics, developed.

We cannot infer that the priests just sat around in their temples and invented mathematics, though, indeed, there may have been some of that even as early as the Mesopotamian era. Their chief contribution, apart from the fact that they recorded their ideas on stone tablets, was the organization and refinement of the methods and techniques of those people who built the canals and temples, or who studied the stars and planets.

It is easy enough to write off the mathematics of the practical person as rule-of-thumb or cookbook, lacking precision and coherence. Certainly these early engineers used approximate methods—whatever would work—in getting the canals built. Each construction situation was different, and you did the best you could, drawing on experience and ingenuity. The problems were certainly quantitative and thus could be classified as mathematical. The priests abstracted from the experience of these practitioners, and their writings have become what is known as "the mathematical tradition."

Well, practical mathematics or abstract mathematics, we would know nothing about either in the Mesopotamian civilization if the people had not been able to write. The priests began to develop writing out of pictograph art about the middle of the fourth millennium B.C.—the earliest development of writing in world history. In its earliest stage, Sumerian script had about 9,000 crude pictograph symbols and little grammatical complexity. The script was used for temple accounts and contained a numerical notàtion that involved a crude, nonpositional decimal base.

By the next stage in the development of the writing, the pictographs became more conventionalized. They approached ideographs, recognized symbols for ideas, rather than accurate drawings of what they represented. An important phonetic element entered into the writing. So the pictograph of an arrow, for example, came to stand for both *ti*, "arrow," and *ti*, "life." Around 3200 B.C., Sumerian scribes discovered that if they rotated the ideographs ninety degrees they could write from left to right more easily. When they began to make wedge-shaped imprints in the tablets, a technique that was much faster than inscribing pictures with a stylus, Sumerian writing became cuneiform in the literal sense, that is, "wedge-shaped."

Cuneiform was a mixed system in its heyday: instead of the massive growth of the almost purely ideographic Chinese system, it has some 700 symbols. About half of them were phonetic, approaching the idea of an alphabetic system: there were 6 vowel symbols; 97 symbols for open syllables like *di*, *du*, *da*; and 200 symbols for closed syllables like *sun*, *dam*, *har*. And there remained two or three hundred special ideographs.

The system had many ambiguities. For example, a triple

This is said to be a Babylonian map of the world. If so, you can readily see they were a long way from the cartography of Ptolemy.

wedge stroke derived from the pictograph for "mountain" acquired 10 phonetic values and 4 ideographic values. That is, it represented 10 different sound words and 4 different idea words. Conversely, the language sound *gar* could be represented by 14 different symbols, each with a distinct meaning. The ambiguities were resolved partly by context and partly by determinatives, added symbols specifying general word categories—deities, male proper names, countries, birds, and so on.

How complicated this early written language was. Very few people had the time to master it, and, therefore, the forms of knowledge that writing made possible. Mathematics were considered mysterious and a part of state power. A note at the end of an astronomical tablet from Uruk gives an indication of this mystery:

> Computation according to the wisdom of Anship, the secret of the deity, the guarded knowledge of the expert. The informed may show it to the informed; the uninformed may not see it. It belongs to the forbidden things of Any, Eniii and Ra, the great Gods.

Schools were established in connection with the temples, originally to train temple and palace clerks. Through the centuries, however, the schools became more secular, and a class of professional scholars emerged—men who spent their lives studying mathematics and astronomy or preserving and adding to the creative literature. Vast libraries grew up around the schools, and word lists, which had been originated to train students in the written vocabulary, grew into inventories of the culture. Botanical and medical knowledge, the legal system, history and mythology, their geographical notion of the world, all were committed to the lists on the clay tablets. Scribes who did not become full-time scholars became merchants or architects.

Of the 500,000 which are now in Western centers, some 300 purely mathematical tablets have been translated. Most of these come from the "old Babylonian" period—about the time of Hammurabi (1800–1600 b.c.e.) —so you can see that there

Otto Neugebauer, a contemporary scholar, deciphered the inscriptions on many Babylonian tablets, including this one. Neugebauer's work has made Babylonian mathematical methods known for the first time, at least in modern history. Babylonian algebra was certainly well advanced compared to the efforts of the later Egyptians, Greeks, and Romans. Courtesy Scripta Mathematica.

is a substantial period of development of mathematical methods as a background to what is written on the clay.

The Sumerians had been conquered by invaders from the north some five hundred years before this, and these conquerors then succumbed to people from the south. After the time of Hammurabi there was a long period of disorder, followed by the "new Babylonian" period of the Seleucid in about 300 B.C. Rulers of this era were descended from one of the generals in the army of Alexander the Great. Another large group of clay texts comes from this "new Babylonian" period.

The "old Babylonians" calculated with a positional number system in the base sixty. It is interesting to speculate on how this base-sixty system developed from the nonpositional decimal system of the ancient Sumerians. Various theories have been advanced, including one that points up the importance of sixty

This version of the Babylonian tablet shows more clearly the char-
acters imprinted on the clay with a stylus. The Babylonians (more
generally, the Mesopotamians) used a positional scale of notation,
of sorts, based on sixty. You find vestiges remaining in our sub-
divisions of the hour and of the degree. Courtesy Scripta Mathematica.

in the figuring of time and angles. It seems more likely that angles (and they were much used in astronomy) were divided into
sixty minutes and the minutes into sixty seconds because the
number system should have been geared to the inclinations of
the astronomer.

For whatever reason, the Babylonians used a sexagesimal
system, which fortunately did not involve sixty different number-symbols. The numerals apparently were built upon the older
decimal base.

We take the zero so much for granted that we find it difficult to imagine doing any arithmetic at all without one. We
could, as apparently the earlier Babylonians did, leave a space to
indicate that there were none of that particular power of sixty.
Thus, interpretation of the mathematical tablets generally depended upon deduction, from the context of the calculation.

A square root technique, which is speculatively attributed to the Babylonians, is much like one credited to Hero, the Greek mathematician of the late Alexandrian period. Hero could well have had access to the results and, possibly, the methods of the Babylonians.

Much ado is made these days about the fact that the square root of 2 is irrational. That is, it cannot be represented as the ratio of two whole numbers. And even rather youthful scholars are exposed to a proof, which dates to the time of the Greeks, that this is so. By contrast, the Babylonian mathematician, or user of mathematics, if you prefer, apparently was not concerned about proofs. Mathematics for him was a practical tool, and he was satisfied with being able to make that tool as accurate as he wanted.

This was no mean feat, particularly when you think about the awkward notation that the Babylonians must have had. Here's a worked-out example from one of the tablets that may give you an idea of how the student of engineering and mathematics went about solving a problem. Just for the record: one cubit=about 20 inches; one gar=6.0 cubits; one sar=the area of a square of a gar on a side.

The problem: "A cistern is 10 gar square and 10 gar deep. I emptied out its water. With its water, how much field did I irrigate to a depth of 1 cubit?"

The solution:

1. Put aside 10 and 10 which form the square.
2. Put aside 10, the depth of the cistern.
3. And put aside 0, 0, 10, the depth of the water that irrigated the field
4. Take the reciprocal of 0, 0, 10, the depth of the water that irrigated the field, and the resulting 6, 0 multiply by 10, the depth of the cistern, and the result is 1, 0, 0.
5. The 1, 0, 0 keep in your head.

6. Square 10, which formed the square, and the result is 1, 40.
7. Multiply 11, 40 by 1, 0, 0 which you are keeping in your head. I irrigated 1, 4, 0, 0, 0 ser field.

This example does point up the kind of problem that they considered important. Other examples that appear on the surviving tablets involve canal building, taxation, inheritance, and interest. Each example is worked out independently, that is, there are no attempts at generalization. The mathematically inclined did work out tables to expedite the calculations in some cases. In particular, they had extensive tables of reciprocals, since apparently they used multiplication by the reciprocal for division. In fact, some people have suggested that the base sixty was chosen by the Babylonians because more reciprocals "come out even" in that base than in base ten.

The explanation seems a bit farfetched, particularly when you consider the advantages in time and effort of dividing directly in base ten. Still, we can view this with the substantial advantage of hindsight and the experience of mathematicians over some thousands of years. What appears obvious even to the mathematically disinclined today may never have occurred to the mathematician of 1600 B.C. Not so incidentally, we might speculate on how they arrived at the tables of reciprocals in the first place.

For whatever its disadvantages, the sexagesimal system continued in favor for thousands of years. The Greeks used it, as did the Moslem mathematicians in the eastern Mediterranean area, and it is even found in medieval European astronomical tables expressed in base sixty.

The Babylonians were involved in moneylending transactions, and this, of course, led to the calculation of interest. For example, if $100 were loaned at 10 per cent interest per year—and compounded annually—the debt would grow at an exponential rate:

	Principal:	Interest:
First year:	100	10
Second year:	110	11
Third year:	121	12.10
Fourth year:	133.10	13.31

You could show this in modern notation as $100 \ (.1+1)^t$, with the t representing the number of years. This kind of financial problem led the Babylonians to develop exponential tables, with principals and interests calculated for various time spans. They apparently moved from such problems to a consideration of a kind of logarithms, but they never got involved to the extent of calculating logarithms to a particular base.

At least one tablet indicates such experimentation, and this suggests that the Babylonian mathematicians did not devote all their efforts to practical problems and special cases. Another bit of evidence involves the right-triangle relationship.

This relationship—that the square on the hypotenuse of a right triangle is equal to the sum of the squares on the two sides—has turned up in China and Egypt also, and its initial recognition probably came from the very practical consideration of constructing a square corner. Now, it is one thing to note that, if you make a triangle with sides of 3, 4, and 5 units respectively, two sides will form a "square corner." And you might muddle about and find that 5, 12, 12 and 8, 15, 17 triangles give the same effect. (Though at that you are beginning to play with mathematics for its own sake, since the 3, 4, 5 triangle would suffice for practical purposes.)

The dabbler in numbers might even notice that $5^2+12^2=13^2$ and $8^2+15^2=17^2$.

If he was sufficiently clever at arithmetic, he would probably experiment with other combinations, and note that $20^2+21^2=29^2$ and, possibly $7^2+24^2=25^2$.

See how far he is already from the practical problem of constructing a square corner?

At such a point, this number juggler might very well tire of his trial-and-error approach and return to more practical matters, such as cisterns and compound interest, or look for an easier way to generate these triples of numbers, so that if you square one of them add it to the square of another, you get, as a sum, the square of the third. Why not organize the evidence:

Odd number	Even number	Odd number
3	4	5
5	12	13
15	8	17
21	20	29
7	24	25

By the time he got this all neatly stamped out with wedges on clay, he would realize the odd numbers fitted into a pattern.

Odd number	Even number	Odd number
$3=4-1$	4	$5=4+1$
$5=9-4$	12	$13=9+4$
$15=16-1$	8	$17=16+1$
$21=25-4$	20	$29=25+4$
$7=16-9$	24	$25=16+9$

And see that all those numbers he was adding and subtracting were square numbers and were related to the even numbers also. And he would go on to calculate other triples from the same pattern:

$$7^2-4^2 \qquad 2\cdot7\cdot4 \qquad 7^2+4^2$$
$$8^2-3^3 \qquad 2\cdot8\cdot3 \qquad 8^2+3^2$$

or if you prefer the base-sixty notation:

$$(1, 5), \quad (1, 12), \quad (1, 37)$$

which is one triple that appeared in a table of such.

The triples (which are now called "Pythagorean triples") suggested in one of the Babylonian tables must have been arrived at with the aid of some pattern or formula. The first five lines of the table show

1, 59	2, 49
56, 7	3, 12, 1
1, 16, 41	1, 50, 49
3, 31, 49	5, 9, 1
1, 5	1, 37

Evidently the relationship was thought to be so obvious that the writer didn't bother to list the third numbers of the triples.

Anyway, the existence of such tables shows that the Babylonians were interested in number relationships beyond the merely practical mathematics. Since the 300 or so mathematical tablets must represent only a small part of the Babylonian results, it may be possible that Greek number theory and "algebra" owe much to earlier Babylonian efforts, as does Greek geometry to that of the Egyptians.

In the thirteen hundred years between the Old Babylonian era and the Seleucid, there was apparently little mathematical progress made in the land between the two rivers, though some scribes in the latter era used a dot as a zero. This notation seems to have been used only infrequently, and the critical idea of the zero neither caught on in Mesopotamia nor was transmitted to the West.

The striking advance between the two Babylonian periods was in astronomy. Before 500 B.C. the Babylonians had some idea of solar and lunar eclipses and of planetary motion. They used a lunar calendar intercalated seven times every nineteen years (quite an accurate approximation) and a zodiac of twelve times thirty degrees for fixing solar and planetary motion. Their observations probably were made by lines of sight, for no astronomical devices have been found by archaeologists in Mesopotamia.

Between 500 and 400 the astronomer-mathematicians of the temples applied their mathematics to this crude astronomy with considerable success. They calculated the length of the solar year as

$$12, 22, 8, 53, 20$$

lunar months, developed a complete theory of the moon's movement and a partial theory for the movement of the planets.

Their astronomy was based on no known visual model—which makes it consistent with their nongeometric approach to mathematics. Nowhere, except in very old and incomplete texts, did the Babylonians speculate about what the universe actually looked like. At the same time that the Greeks were arguing the

Note the efforts at perspective in this Assyrian bas-relief. The representation does seem to have depth, and you might contrast this with artistic efforts of the early Christian era, and later, where no insight into perspective is evident. The techniques were not revived until the fourteenth and fifteenth centuries; finally mastered by such artists as Albrecht Dürer, and eventually mathematized in the nineteenth century.

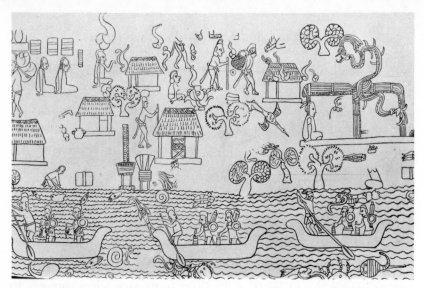

Not all Mesopotamian art showed insight into perspective, as did that war scene shown earlier. However lacking in depth, this drawing shows many facets of the day-to-day life of those early people in the land between the two rivers.

relative merits of the earth-centered and sun-centered models, the Babylonians were simply developing mathematical descriptions of celestial movements.

Before Otto Neugebauer's recent cuneiform research, it was believed that Babylonian mathematics had grown out of number mysticism and that Babylonian astronomy had grown out of astrology. Classical sources tell of the skill of the "Chaldean" (i.e., Mesopotamian) astrologers, and an old belief is that Babylonian astronomy owed its excellence to good observation, made easier in a desert land where the night sky is so clear and bright. In fact, the night sky in the Middle Eastern desert is often obscured by sandstorms, and the horizon, the point of reference for most Babylonian observations, can be hazy.

Although the later Babylonians put a great deal of faith in their ability to "read" the stars, we have no reason to believe that astrological problems were of the sort to stimulate mathematical astronomy. According to the cuneiform evidence, the astronomy of the Old Babylonian period was just adequate for maintaining the calendar, on which the irrigation system supporting the civilization depended. Astronomy had little effect on mathematics, but mathematics made astronomy bloom without any vast improvement in observational techniques, and gave to astronomy its own nongeometric imprint.

There was some numerology in Mesopotamia. Every god possessed·a number, and Anu, the supreme god, had the perfect number, 60. Every character in the cuneiform syllabary had a number attached to it, so a man's name could be given a numerical value. Thus Sargon II inscribed on the walls of a city he built, "I build the circuit of the wall of 116,283 cubits, the number of my name." But the Babylonian mathematicians seem not to have been concerned about the properties of numbers in themselves. Nor, apparently, were they trying to work out answers with sacred implications, as the Maya may have been doing with their calendar round.

Little is known about the social implications of Mesopotamian mathematics. The scribes, priests, and astronomer-mathematicians were probably closely related—perhaps a distinct class. And, the ruler's lack of divinity may have meant that the priestly class was more independent of political authority than were the "intellectuals" of Peru or Egypt. Nor was Mesopotamia ever a single centralized empire as China was. The culture had a dark and disorderly philosophy of warring gods, but not a restricting official philosophy like Confucianism.

Still, after its early creative burst in the Old Babylonian period, Mesopotamian mathematics stagnated for the rest of its history. Major mathematical advances, like scientific ones, seem to require a certain indefinable social atmosphere *and* a number of individual geniuses. Apparently neither existed in Mesopotamia after the Old Babylonian period.

5

PRACTICAL PROBLEMS
ALONG THE NILE

It is possible to look at Egyptian mathematics from two points of view: to see the marvelous formulas that the Greeks didn't understand until the time of Archimedes, the beginnings of trigonometry, and the remarkable accuracy of their construction; or to see mere empirical results: simple, practical, and of little intellectual value. Both points of view are valid.

Let us look first of all at the Egyptians' practical accomplishments. They developed a system of land surveying which worked. (Herodotus, the Greek historian and geographer, attributed the beginning of Western mathematics to the Egyptian need for resurveying the land each spring, following the flooding of the Nile.) Never mind the theory, the system worked. The Egyptians, after building pyramids for a few thousand years, concluded that the volume could be computed by multiplying the area of the base by the height, and that result by one-third. Of course they didn't prove that such a formula would work for all pyramids, but they knew very well that it had sufficed for the pyramids with which they had had experience. They knew that a triangle with sides of three, four, and five units would give them a right angle. And there was no need to talk about the square on the hypotenuse.

Admirers of the Greeks, on the other hand, regard mathematics as a logical system. We begin with certain assumptions (axioms, postulates) about the things with which we are dealing—numbers, points, lines, etc.—and then we prove, logically, that certain properties follow from these assumptions. Thus, for *every* right triangle, the square on the hypotenuse is equal to the sum of the squares on the two sides. Also, if two sides of a triangle are of equal length, the angles opposite these sides are equal.

Currently there is a sentiment toward glorifying this point of view and, in terms of history, emphasizing the Greek contributions and writing off the efforts of the Egyptians. This willingness to forget the Egyptian mathematics is due in part to the dearth of information on the subject. There are just two significant sources—the Rhind (or Ahmes) papyrus and the Moscow papyrus—and it is reasonable, if not scientific, to speculate on what has been lost.

One can expect to find written down more of what the scholars have to say on mathematics than what the builders and others who are practically inclined have to say. Granted that many of the original Greek works have been lost, we still have much more to go on than we do for the Egyptians. Greek geometry—and it was a remarkable intellectual system—owes much to the practical work of both the Egyptians and the Babylonians. There is evidence that Thales and Pythagoras, two of the great early Greek mathematicians, spent some time in Egypt and may have brought back reports on Egyptian methods.

There is a third point of view: that of mathematics as an avocation—a hobby—or something to play around with and have fun with. As a social factor, this point of view could be significant, since more people would be involved. Some important results have come from outstanding amateurs, but the notion seems never to have been generally accepted. It is unlikely that the average citizen of ancient Greece or Egypt counted mathematics among his hobbies.

Having, I hope, placed the Egyptian mathematics in perspective vis-à-vis the contributions of other cultures, I'll try to establish something of a cultural context for the mathematics before going on to the particulars.

Egyptian civilization was more tranquil than was that of Mesopotamia. There were geographic and political reasons for this. While the Tigris-Euphrates Valley was a maze of unreliable rivers and canals, without natural boundaries between the hostile city-states, Egypt was a single strip of land between the Nile and the desert. The river flooded the fields regularly every spring, just after the star Sirius rose off the horizon at sunrise. The climate was temperate.

Egypt, all through its history, was divided into Upper Egypt, the south, and Lower Egypt, the north. Lower Egypt was, in fact, more like Mesopotamia—a delta area. Upper Egypt was a country about ten miles wide, following the Nile through the Sahara. According to Egyptian legend, the two lands were first united around 3200 B.C. by Menes—also called Narmer—who is supposed to have created his capital city, Memphis, at the point where Upper and Lower Egypt met. The "White Walls" of Memphis stood, the Egyptians believed, on land reclaimed by a diversion of the Nile River. So the first Pharaoh of united Egypt was closely associated with the Nile and with irrigation projects. He was believed to bring rain as well as river water to his people.

The Pharaoh, in contrast to the Mesopotamian king, was a living deity—an incarnation of the sky god Horus. The Narmer tablet, one of the oldest Egyptian stone documents, shows the Pharaoh under the sign of Horus, represented as a hawk, sacrificing a captive. On one side Narmer is dressed as a medicine man—a giver of health—and on the other side are scenes of Narmer's military victories. As a living god, he was far above all the rest of mankind. He was the source of his country's power and welfare.

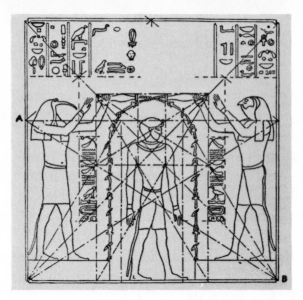

The original caption for this sketch of an Egyptian bas-relief notes that the lines show "the application of the design planning methods used by the artists of that period." I would qualify this to read "hypothesized by some to have been used . . ." for the theory of dynamic symmetry is far from being generally accepted. Courtesy Scripta Mathematica.

But while the Pharaoh was a divine being, the heir to the god of creation, the Egyptian civilization did not have quite the authoritarian atmosphere of the empire of the Inca. After the early dynasties, Egyptian art began to show figures other than the Pharaoh. In particular, and perhaps inevitably, a class of bureaucrats was rising in power and prestige.

The power of the official class was based on its learning. A boy was sent to school at the age of four, and spent twelve years learning hieroglyphic script and other subjects. He learned more or less by rote, copying parts of the classic texts and long word-lists of geographic names, articles of trade, religious feasts, and mathematical terms. An old text, *The Satire on Trades*, admonishes the student to continue his difficult studies, for a scribe's life is so much more pleasant and rewarding than any other occupation.

When a boy graduated from scribal school, he was qualified

for most of the high posts in the kingdom. The army, the treasury, the palace, and the priesthood all had positions for him. He could remain a village letter writer or rise to the office of the Pharaoh's private secretary. The patron saint of the scribes was Imhotep, a figure who probably had some historical reality. Legend has it that Imhotep was an adviser to Zoser, one of the most dynamic of the early Pharaohs. He is credited with inventing architectural techniques for stone, making the pyramid age possible, and with innovations in medicine, mathematics, and magic (though possibly not in that order of significance). Imhotep was remembered for thousands of years in Egypt, for he represented the archetype of the learned man and his achievements.

The earliest surviving example of Egyptian written language dates to about the time of Egypt's unification. It appears to be pictographic, but was in fact ideographic. That is, the pictographics had already become conventionalized. It may be that Egyptian writing did not pass through the early stages of development as did that of the Chinese and Mesopotamian, but might have been artificially created at the time of the unification by someone familiar with the idea of writing. Cuneiform writing had existed in Sumeria for several hundred years, and the idea may have been transmitted. This hypothetical inventor of Egyptian script apparently did not actually know any cuneiform, and he had to work out his own system from the beginning.

Hieroglyphic writing became more phonetic as it developed, and finally was much closer to an alphabetic system than was the cuneiform. Signs existed only for consonants, and the scribe had to be able to supply the vowel sounds when reading the text aloud. The script finally had about seventy-five signs for sound units with two consonants, and thirty for uniconsonantal sounds. Hieroglyphics remained complex, however. Part of this complexity seems to have been the fault of the priests and other writers who often drew in archaic ideographs alongside the phonetic script.

One of the most exciting events of nineteenth-century classical archaeology occurred when the French scholar Champollion deciphered hieroglyphics for the modern world, making possible most of what we know today about the Egyptian civilization.

The Egyptians had a written numerical notation as long as they had a literary script. The early notation was nonpositional, decimal, and must have been useful only so long as needs were confined to the indicating of numbers. There was a new symbol for each higher order than the power of ten.

The system had limitations, of the same kind that those known as "Roman numerals" have, and it is not surprising that, when transactions requiring numerical description became a bit more involved, the Egyptians began to develop a more workable system.

This cumbersome notation did force the Egyptians to develop some unusual arithmetical techniques. Among other things they reduced multiplication to successive doublings and addition.

The best known Egyptian mathematical text is the Rhind papyrus, which was written about the middle of the second millennium B.C. According to A'h-mose, the scribe who wrote it, this papyrus is a copy of an older text of about 1825 B.C. The Rhind papyrus begins with a treatment of fractions and computations with fractions—and people have been having trouble with them ever since. The Egyptians used only unit fractions, with the exception of two-thirds, for which they had a special symbol.

The papyrus begins with a table of what amounts to equivalents in unit fractions for fractions of the form 2/n. For example (and, remember, things look a lot better in modern notation) :

$$\tfrac{2}{5}=\tfrac{1}{3}+\tfrac{1}{15}$$
$$\tfrac{2}{7}=\tfrac{1}{4}+\tfrac{1}{28}$$
$$\tfrac{2}{9}=\tfrac{1}{4}+\tfrac{1}{18}$$
$$\tfrac{2}{11}=\tfrac{1}{6}+\tfrac{1}{66}$$
$$\tfrac{2}{13}=\tfrac{1}{8}+\tfrac{1}{52}+\tfrac{1}{104}$$

down to

$$\tfrac{2}{101}=\tfrac{1}{101}+\tfrac{1}{202}+\tfrac{1}{303}+\tfrac{1}{606}$$

At that, there was a certain reasonableness to the arguments given by A'h-mose for some of these entries. For example, in discussing the first entry—2 is what part of 5—he notes that "1 and ⅔ is ⅓ of 5, and the other ⅓ is ¹⁄₁₅ of 5."

The early Egyptians obviously did a lot of number juggling in working out such tables of results. And maybe these tables were even useful.

Other problems in the Rhind papyrus involve land measurement and basic geometric figures. The displayed geometry is about on a level with that of the Babylonians, though the Egyptians did not have the algebraic knowledge of the Babylonians, to facilitate the expression of geometric results. There are formulas given (not all of them correct) for the areas of rectangles, triangles, and "truncated triangles" (trapezoids). The Egyptians used specific examples, as did the Babylonians and Chinese. All had a common handicap—the lack of really versatile notation.

A'h-mose gave the area of a circle as the square of 8/9 times the diameter. This means they used $256/81 \approx 3.16$ for the circumference/diameter ratio, which is not a bad approximation, at that.

The Rhind papyrus includes observations on mathematical properties of pyramids, including a relation, *seqet*, "which makes the nature of a pyramid." The seqet is the ratio of half the length of the base of a pyramid to the height—what we now call the cotangent of the angle of the side of the pyramid—and it does determine the shape of the figure.

The Moscow papyrus, written about the same time as the Rhind papyrus, contains some remarkable results. One was a formula for the volume of a truncated pyramid, which implies that the Egyptians had a formula for the volume of a whole pyramid. The Greeks developed such a formula only after they had worked out their sophisticated mathematical technique of "exhaustion." The Egyptians must have worked their formula out empirically, but it worked.

They also apparently used the equivalent of the formula:

$$2\pi r^2$$

for the surface area of a hemisphere. The Greeks weren't up to this until the time of Archimedes.

But, with these exceptions, the problems of the two surviving Egyptian mathematical papyri are much simpler mathematically than were those of Mesopotamian tablets. They usually involved such matters as the division of loaves, field acreage, volume of granaries, the herdsman's produce, or the exchange of bread and beer.

At some later date, the cumbersome lotus-flower-scroll notation was abandoned in Egypt in favor of a decimal system that was positional to an extent. The Phoenicians may have contributed to this development, which was adopted about 500 B.C. by the Greeks, who used their letters, with amplifying marks, for numerals. There is quite a lapse, then, between the time of the surviving Egyptian mathematical papyri and the adoption by the Greeks of the Egyptian system of numeration, and it seems not completely unreasonable to speculate that in the interim the Egyptians used their improved notation to amplify upon their empirical results—which improvements might have been of interest to the Greeks.

The Egyptians used several different calendars. One was

used for the agricultural cycle and was based, not surprisingly, on the annual flooding of the Nile. They also had a civil calendar with twelve thirty-day months and a five-day period at the end of the year. The civil calendar was not intercalated at all, so it slowly fell behind the astronomical year. It was adopted by the Greek astronomers, however, and eventually the Roman calendar, instituted by Julius Caesar, was patterned after this Egyptian civil calendar. These calendars were intercalated.

The Egyptians named the fixed constellations and divided those along the zodiac—which rose at different hours as the seasons changed—into thirty-six decans. This gave them a star clock from which they could tell time at night. This reckoning of time was transformed into twelve night and twelve complementary daylight hours—and from these we have our division of the day into twenty-four hours.

The Egyptians also had sundials of sorts, which determined the hour according to the shadow cast by the sun. The only other known astronomical instrument was a split palm and a plumb line that they may have used for taking lines of sight on celestial objects. They evidently had no systematic theory to account for the movements of the sun, moon, and planets, and, while they did observe and record eclipses, they could not explain them astronomically.

The most impressive monuments to the Egyptian civilization are, of course, the pyramids. Most were built during the Old Kingdom (about 2500 B.C.). They were intended to facilitate the Pharaoh's entrance into the Land of the Dead, to assure his transformation from Horus to Osiris. In form they were modeled on the solar symbol of the sun god, Ra, which was actually conical in shape—the square pyramids were evidently a practical compromise. The shape is also associated with the primeval mound above the waters, from which the world was created—the hieroglyphic symbol for pyramid and primeval mound was the same.

The largest and most perfect of the pyramids is the Great Pyramid at Gizeh, originally 451 feet high, with its four faces each having an area of more than four acres. Just for the record, the Great Pyramid is said to have taken about 100,000 men twenty years to build, and involved the stacking of some 2,300,000 two-and-a-half-ton blocks. Probably a lot of people complained about the cost, but the project did provide a lot of jobs, and it might be described as being "good for the economy."

The accuracy of the construction is quite remarkable. The four sides of the base are all within four inches of 756.8 feet in length. The orientation of the base to the cardinal points of the compass is not off on any one edge by more than 5'28". Try to do that with two-and-a-half-ton blocks. The 75-inch-long edges of the blocks do not deviate from a straight line by more than 1/1000 of an inch, and the foundation of the pyramid is at all points within one-half inch of true level.

These specifications give an idea of the extraordinary craftsmanship of the builders of the Great Pyramid, but they do not imply any mathematical competence beyond some practical geometry and what is shown in the mathematical papyri. Still, they were doing all right for 2500 B.C. People who have been intrigued with number mysticism of sorts have attempted to find all kinds of symbolism in the pyramids. One notion is that the Egyptians were aware of the special ratio, called much later "the golden section," and that they built this into their pyramids. The golden section is that of dividing a line segment so that the ratio of the smaller part to the larger part is equal to the ratio of the larger part to the entire segment. One approximation is 1.618, or its reciprocal, depending on how you look at the section. Looking closely at the statistics on pyramids, I find no very close approximations to the golden section, and I suspect that, if the Egyptians were inclined toward that kind of thing, their accuracy here would have been on a par with their accuracy in other respects.

Others have suggested that the Egyptians were aware of a very good approximation to the circumference/diameter ratio, and that they built this into the pyramids. Again, the expounders of the theory did not bother to confuse the issue with facts. A subsequent checking of data revealed no better approximation, and even this may have been mere chance, than that given in the papyri—about 3.16.

At that, some of the construction techniques of the Egyptians were probably more direct than mathematical. The almost perfect level of the base was probably achieved by ancient field-level technique: a mud wall was built around the area, water let in, and the base cut at a certain small distance below the perfect level of the water.

Their probable method for orienting the pyramid to true north was a little more sophisticated, though it involved very little astronomical knowledge. A ring or wall was constructed with an absolutely level top to act as a horizon. A star was sighted in the northern part of the sky, made just as the star lifted off the artificial horizon of the ring. Then the same star was sighted again as it set on the artificial horizon. The angle of the two sightings is bisected to give true north. The Egyptians probably used a plumb line for bisecting the angle.

In the final reckoning, then, the recorded mathematical accomplishments of the Egyptians were not significant. If we assume, for the minute, that what is recorded is a reasonable indication of the total, how can we account for the Egyptians' failure to study mathematics for its own sake—as an intellectual pursuit? It may have been the fact that the supreme political ruler, the Pharaoh, was considered divine, and those around him—scribes and priests—who might have worked in this field were too subordinated in the social structure to do more than keep accounts and develop an official religion. This would be a simplification, however, for the Egyptian intelligentsia had some prestige and independence after the earlier dynasties. But, like the Chinese civilization, Egypt found its form at an early date, and then lost its intellectual dynamism. Egypt might have been the most pleasant of the early civilizations, but it was not the most intellectually stimulating.

On the other hand, I still am convinced that Western mathematics owes a substantial debt to the Egyptian practitioners.

6

INTERLUDE:
THE WEST BEFORE THE GREEKS

As of 1500 B.C.E., both the Egyptian and Mesopotamian civilizations had found their distinctive forms and developed mathematics that served their practical needs. Egypt and Mesopotamia were aware of one another—they sometimes fought and sometimes traded—but though there was some borrowing of artistic motifs and technological processes, in mathematics the two civilizations were entirely independent of each other. China's development was just beginning.

In terms of high culture and mathematics, Europe until the middle of the first millennium B.C. was far behind the civilizations of the Near East. European prehistory is known in some detail, though in the absence of writing we can only learn so much from archaeological remains. The archaeologist Marshack has analyzed cave drawings and other rock scratchings all over Europe and discovered that tallies of twenty-nine or thirty (twenty-nine or thirty similar marks on a rock, for instance) occur more often than would be the case if they were entirely random statistically. He concludes that, for at least thirty thousand years, men were making counts of the days in a lunar period—men were estimating months.

An English engineer, Alexander Thom, has studied prehistoric stone circles in England and Scotland and suggested that they demonstate some implicit geometric knowledge. A

The mystery of Stonehenge has been only recently explained. The huge stones, set in circular and elliptical patterns, apparently (and the arguments are most convincing) constituted a solar observatory.

large number of them are perfect circles, a simple construction, but some are fairly accurate ellipses. Most intriguing is a group of "circles" of apparently irregular shape. One segment of this type of stone ring is circular, while the remainder is an irregular shape. Since the ratio between the diameter and circumference on one group is 3.06, and on another 2.96, Thom speculates that they were constructed in order to make a perfect 3 (the biblical value, incidentally) a more satisfactory value than 3.1415926535.

Stone circles in England are just one part of a widespread phase of building with large stones in Western Europe about 2500 B.C. Megalithic tombs and temples, whose meaning can only be guessed at, are found all over Spain, France, and Scandinavia as well as Great Britain. The best known of the stone constructions is Stonehenge, four concentric circles of stones on the Salisbury Plain in England. The very existence of Stonehenge indicates some sort of hierarchy, headed by a priest or a chief, which could organize and direct large forces of human labor. Some of the larger stones were brought hundreds of miles by sea and land from the mountains of Wales, and the total

labor for erecting the monument has been conservatively esti-
mated at 1,500,000 man days (this is, however, under one-
hundredth the labor expended on the Great Pyramid at Gizeh).

We have no way of knowing the true purpose of Stonehenge, but some suggestive work has been done by Gerald Hawkins, author of *Stonehenge Decoded.* Hawkins has unearthed
an old quotation from Diodorus' *History of the Ancient World*
(ca. 50 B.C.) which may mean that the Britons worshiped the
sun and moon and that their priests had derived some astronomical knowledge from this worship:

> The moon as viewed from this island appears
> to be put a little distance from the Earth and
> to have on it prominences like those on Earth,
> which are visible to the eye. The account is
> also given that the God visits the island every
> 19 years, the period in which the return of the
> stars to the same place in the heavens is accomplished. . . .
> There is also on the island both a magnificent sacred precinct of
> Apollo (Sun) and a notable temple . . . and the supervisors are
> called Boreadae. And the succession to these positions is
> always kept in their family.

Hawkins has fed the positions of key stones at Stonehenge
into a computer programmed with astronomical data. He has
come up with correlations implying that the stones might have
been used for lines of sight on sunrise and sunset, and moonrise
and moonset, on the solstices and possibly the equinoxes. Hawkins suggests, in an intriguing argument, that Stonehenge was
a "primitive computer" for predicting periods when lunar or
solar eclipses were likely to occur. The nineteen-year cycle
mentioned by Diodorus is a useful one for lunar eclipses, though
the actual cycle is between eighteen and nineteen years. This a
period of 19+19+18=56 years for three cycles is more accurate, and this is just the number in the outer ring of holes, which
could have served as a counting device. Also, two of the inner

*If you need to be convinced of the impressiveness of Stonehenge,
perhaps this picture will help. Almost as impressive, though, were
the empirical methods applied by these builders to their problems
in astronomy. I suspect that only a mystic would appreciate why
people would go to all this in order to predict such as the equinoxes
and solstices.*

rings of holes may number twenty-nine and thirty—they could
have been day counters for the month.

Hawkins' argument, as he himself admits, is speculative.
It can be simplified slightly, leaving out the esoteric eclipse
theory, to an intercalating interpretation, for the ten-year and
fifty-six-year cycles would be useful for adjusting the lunar and
solar years as for predicting eclipses. Diodorus' quotation, in
any case, suggests a religious view of time like the Maya, based
on a recurring cycle. When the heavens had returned to their

The ancients who built Stonehenge did not have the advantages afforded by equipment such as this derrick. I have found, as yet, no adequate explanation of how the top stone was originally placed there.

initial position, the god returned to his people.

At the period of the last building phase of Stonehenge, around 1500 B.C., trade routes extended from Great Britain through Central Europe into the Aegean area. Amber and weapons found their way from the Aegean to the south of England and Ireland; we can only speculate about accompanying transmission of astronomical and mathematical ideas.

The Minoan civilization, a society influenced by Egypt and Mesopotamia but a civilization in its own right, held political and cultural sway over the eastern Mediterranean area at this time. The Minoans seem to have been organized on an Oriental model, with a governmental hierarchy and some advanced architectural techniques including indoor plumbing. But the layouts of Minoan palaces are quite different from those of the palaces of Egypt or Babylonia, and Minoan power was based on control of the sea rather than on large armies.

The Minoans had a written language named "Linear B" by the first excavator on Crete, Sir Arthur Evans. Linear B looks at first glance like hieroglyphics, but it defied all attempts at deciphering until shortly after 1950, when Michael Ventris, a Greek scholar, approached it on the assumption that it was a precursor to Greek rather than a variant of Egyptian. The script was soon broken, and our picture of the old Aegean civilization has been much extended.

On mainland Greece, for example, the closely related Mycenaean civilization, which also used Linear B, had a feudal organization. A priest-king of the type familiar to us from Western Asia and Central America controlled the west coast of the mainland from Pylos, a city that fell into ruin after the end of the Mycenaean age. Pylos received tribute from two provinces, "the seven" and "the nine," the names referring to the number of tribute palaces in each province. The King of Pylos had an efficient bureaucracy of officials and scribes who managed the tribute and the redistribution of wealth in a manner similar to the temple management in Mesopotamia. The number system of Linear B is an additive decimal notation like the earliest Egyptian system.

Mycenaean scribes added and subtracted accurately, and they could manage some higher computational problems. One palace record at Pylos tells of the tribute quantities for a number of villages. Each village's total contribution is different, but the ratio between the six different commodities remains the same in each case:

$$7:7:2:3:1\frac{1}{2}:150$$

The Mycenaeans had three systems of weights and measures: weight measure, dry measure, and wet measure. A ration statement from Knossos, at a later time when Pylos had political control of Crete, tells us that the allotment of food to men, women, and children was according to the whole number ratio $5:2:1$. A slave received half the daily ration of a free man. It may have been this sort of practical calculation that lay at the root of the base-sixty number system in Mesopotamia.

The tablets of Pylos were written in unbaked clay and would not have survived had it not been for the catastrophic invasion that struck the Aegean area sometime in the twelfth century B.C. The palace at Pylos was overwhelmed and burned, and the embers baked the tablets that were stored in the basement. We are not entirely sure who the invaders were, but they have been labeled the Dorians after the dominant language group in mainland Greece. The Dorians probably came down from the north, bringing with them an iron technology they had learned from the Hittites of Anatolia. The Hittite Empire fell to invaders about this time. Much was made in nineteenth-century archaeology of the stone, copper-bronze, and iron ages, but these are no longer considered such fundamental divisions of prehistory. Nevertheless, possession of iron weapons did give the Dorians an advantage over the Bronze Age Greeks and might have had something to do with the success of the invasion.

When the Mycenaean-Minoan civilization fell, a vacuum of power occurred in the eastern Mediterranean. One of the peoples to take advantage of this was the Phoenicians. They were good sailors and merchants, and from their home ports of Byblos, Sidon, and Tyre they colonized most of the Mediterranean seaboard in the period 1000–800 B.C. The Phoenician colony of Carthage was more significant in ancient history than Phoenicia proper, for its sphere of influence was to conflict with Rome's in later centuries.

The greatest contribution of the Phoenicians was their spread of the first alphabetic system of writing in world history. As we have seen, both cuneiform and hieroglyphics approached an alphabetic system, but in neither case did the final simplification to one symbol for each speech sound occur. Around 1500 B.C., the area of north Palestine was in an intellectual ferment. The Babylonian and Egyptian civilizations were both dealing with domestic problems, and Palestine, a crossroads of influence from both civilizations, was left to its own devices. An alphabet was devised by the northern Semites and taken over by the Phoenicians, who worked out a set of twenty-two symbols for their own language—consonant sounds only. The Greeks later borrowed the alphabet from the Phoenicians, adding vowel symbols, and our modern system is a descendant of Greek and Roman writing.

A true alphabet ranks with a positional numerical notation as a fundamental cultural break-through. Both are radical simplifications that at one stroke make the literary and the mathematical easier to learn and to manipulate. But though the two inventions are comparable, though they both require the sudden intuition that comes only to an occasional genius, they do not necessarily happen at the same time—they are not both associated with any cultural "level." In China, a positional base-ten system was an early invention, but a phonetic alphabet was never developed. In the West, outside of Mesopotamia, phonetic writing emerged about fifteen hundred years before a truly positional notation was used.

At the same time that the Phoenicians were expanding into the western Mediterranean, the Greeks, as distinct from the Mycenaeans, were spreading through the Aegean and setting up their own colonies on the shores of the Mediterranean. After the Dorian invasion from the Balkans into northern Greece (ca. 1150–1100 B.C.) —which may well have been the one that destroyed the Mycenaeans, a number of Greeks left the Greek peninsula and settled on the coast of Asia Minor, an area which they called Ionia. The Homeric poems, the *Iliad* and the *Odyssey*, took shape and were written down, probably for the first time, in the form we know them today, around 700 B.C. But for four hundred years after the Dorian invasion there is a blank in our knowledge of what was happening in Greece, so for want of a better name we call it a "dark age." The two poems mentioned above represent the culmination of a long oral tradition stretching back into the Mycenaean age (an oral tradition that still survives to this day in remote parts of Yugoslavia). When they came out of their "dark age," the Greeks had developed on the Mycenaean ruins a new form of society, one that was not monolithic in the manner of the early civilizations—a society where priests and kings no longer counted for everything.

7

GREEK MATHEMATICS: THE EARLY DISCOVERIES

Herodotus' theory about the origins of geometry was a utilitarian one: mathematics had originated in Egypt to deal with the Nile. Aristotle suggested an alternative theory that was more social. Science could not develop, he said, without a leisure class whose members spent their time thinking instead of working. The priestly scholars of most of the early civilizations were not a class of manual laborers, certainly, but they tended to be subordinated to the state.

Greece in the fifth century B.C. was unique in producing a new kind of scholar, who might be called an intellectual. Any society tries to make sense of the universe. These early intellectuals of classical Greece re-examined and modified their ideas about the world. What we call philosophy is derived from the Greek words *philos*, "lover of," *sophia*, "wisdom."

Mathematics provided a model in this Greek mode of thought as it did for the Chinese world view. But while in China mathematics was a metaphor for the social order, for the harmonious affairs of men, in Greece mathematics was more abstract, and its philosophical role was more purely intellectual. According to Plato, mathematics was the perfect mode of thought, the way to an understanding of the ideal order underlying a reality that only appeared to be real. In the *Republic*, Plato constructs his best-known image of the relation between reality and the ideal. Our knowledge is like the knowledge of men chained in a cave, away from the opening and the light; all that they see of the world are shadows on the wall, and from these shadows they must understand. But mathematics, according to Plato, is a mode of pure understanding, one that does not depend on the faulty evidence of our senses.

I have used the words "Greece" and "Greek" several times and, just for the record, will specify what I mean—for their meaning in the history of mathematics is quite different from their use today. In the early days, seventh and sixth centuries B.C., the Greeks were located over most of the eastern and central portions of the Mediterranean area. The holdings, established as trading centers by a seafaring people, were eventually consolidated and embellished, so that the "Greek" mathematicians number, among others, Thales of Miletus, Pythagoras, at Croton in Italy, Archytas of Tarentum, Euclid at Alexandria, and Archimedes of Syracuse. None of these cities are in mainland Greece.

The cosmopolitan nature of the Greek civilization contributed significantly to the development of this dynamic, intellectually inclined culture. Greece was a melting pot of sorts, but its chief contributions were of the abstract—philosophic, artistic, and mathematical—rather than the more material output of that much later melting pot, the United States. The Greeks of the seventh and sixth centuries B.C. were a particularly mobile people, and that mobility ensured a regular leavening of new ideas and worked against the rigidity of ideas too long held whose continuing validity was never examined critically.

And there must have been a substantial element of chance which contributed to development of the Greek "genius." The Greek thinkers made choices at certain points in their history—that the "real" was not necessarily what you see, for example—

which they then worked out over a period of perhaps a thousand years.

Here we should look at the influence of Greek social forms on the development of philosophy and mathematics. In the centuries when the Greek intellectual tradition was forming, Greece was never submitted to a harsh centralization like the one that crushed the Mohists in China. The history of Greece is full of bloody and often foolish wars, but five hundred years of competition between rival city-states gave the classical Greeks a choice: a Greek citizen could live under monarchy, aristocracy, oligarchy, tyranny, or democracy, and if he did not like the city-state in which he was born, he could emigrate. In this turbulent social atmosphere, self-critical thought was almost a necessity.

Monarchy was never very important in Greek history. In this, Greece differed from the great Eastern civilizations. The most common form of government in the earliest Greek city-states was *aristocracy*, "rule by the best." The noble class of an aristocracy, a group of highborn families, provided the ruling council for a city-state, and the council in turn appointed officials every year to administer the city. Occasionally the wealthier commoners were allowed a popular assembly, where they could vote on specific issues determined by the aristocrats. But the commoners had no real franchise.

In inland agricultural city-states, an aristocracy provided a fairly stable government, but in coastal trading communities, new economic factors made politics more dynamic. A commoner could make a large fortune from overseas trade, but though he might then begin to live like the aristocracy, he could never become an aristocrat himself. *Oligarchy*, "rule by the few," came into being—"the few" could mean "the rich" or could be a negative term used by the newly rich against the old aristocracy. In sixth-century Athens, the aristocrats allowed a mediator, Solon, to write an early code of law, in hopes that legal guarantees would weaken popular dissatisfaction with their elitist rule. But a half century later the tyrant Pisistratus seized power.

The tyrant in classical Greece was often a true reformer. He came into office by force, in opposition to the nobility, and usually had to align himself with the commoners. Eventually the people reacted against the tyrant, but a restored oligarchy could never be so repressive after a tyrant's reforms. In Athens, after Pisistratus and his son had fallen, another political form was devised, *democracy*, "rule by the people."

"Democracy" is a word so variously used in the modern world that the intent of the Greeks—who invented it—is obscured. Democracy did not come into being in Athens by the will of any idealistic social reformer, but because the weaker aristocratic faction, in the political struggle after the fall of the tyrant Cleisthenes, took the people into partnership. Any citizen of classical Athens had a right to serve as an official or to attend assembly for debating or voting. But citizenship belonged to only 40,000 adult males from a peak Athens population of 300,- 000. There were about 60,000 slaves at this time, a large number of aliens without political rights, and at least 150,000 unenfranchised women.

Athenian democracy at least meant political freedom for a certain class, freedom to a unique degree in world history. And the Greeks had extraordinary theological freedom. A man depended as much on his own courage and ingenuity as on the favor of the gods. The more important gods in the complex Greek pantheon had cults, cult priesthoods, and temples, but no national priesthood of the Mesopotamian kind ever took hold in Greece. The Greeks respected the wisdom of the oracle to Apollo at Delphi, but the oracle could be wrong: in 480 B.C., the oracle sensibly and incorrectly predicted the victory of the invading Persians.

In discussing early Greek mathematics, we must take account of later Greek mathematics. Euclid's *Elements* so com-

pletely summed up the earlier Greek achievements that all
works written before it became obsolete. Since the preservation
of a written tradition in the absence of printing was such an ar-
duous task, and since there were so few copies of any one work,
this obsolescence means that almost all the mathematical works
before Euclid have disappeared. There was no reason to continue copying them. So we know these earlier works only
through hearsay.

According to later commentaries, the first great thinker in
Greek history was Thales of Miletus, said to have lived between
624 and 547 B.C. Miletus was the most important city of Ionic
Greece, and a city that considered itself an offshoot of Crete. It
may have been descended from the Minoan civilization in a
more direct way than most of the Greek city-states. Miletus was
in closer contact with Mesopotamia and Egypt than Doric
Greece, by virtue of its position on the mainland of Asia Minor.
The city was a trading center like Athens, with a political history of commercial aristocracy alternating with reformist tyranny.

Thales was one of the Seven Wise Men of Greece, according to the Roman biographer Plutarch, and his wisdom was the
purest—"the rest acquired the reputation of wisdom in politics."
He did dabble in politics upon occasion. He attempted to save
Ionia from the Lydian invasion by proposing a federation of
city-states, and by clever politics he kept Miletus from destruction during the Persian invasion under Cyrus. Thales was capable of business when he put his mind to it—one year he cornered
the olive presses of the region and made a small fortune from his
monopoly. Such circumstances are indeed conducive to a subsequent life of contemplation.

But, according to legend, Thales considered these worldly
activities unimportant. He kept his monopoly for just a year,
since he only wanted to prove the business principle (and make
just a *small* fortune). His real bent, Aristotle says, was philos-

ophy. Thales took a world view that may have been a development of the Babylonian cosmology: the basic element was water, from which everything had emerged. Astronomy and cosmology are concerned with the same subject: Thales was credited by later Greeks with predicting the solar eclipse of May 28, 585 B.C., from astronomical knowledge he had picked up on a trip to Mesopotamia. Proculus claims he journeyed to Egypt to learn geometry. Another report has it that Thales showed the Egyptians how to measure the height of a pyramid from shadows and similar triangles.

Proculus credited Thales with *proofs* of the following propositions:

(1) A circle is bisected by its diameter.
(2) The angles at the base of an isosceles triangle are equal.
(3) If two lines cut across one another, vertical and opposite angles are equal.
(4) If two triangles have two angles and one side equal, the triangles are equal.

These theorems are the most difficult part of the Thales legend to believe, for theorems imply a complete understanding of the axiomatic method, an understanding that would have been most unlikely three hundred years before Euclid. The processes of mathematical *discovery* and mathematical *proof* are entirely different, as I have tried to point out earlier. Crediting Thales with these discoveries is like suggesting that gravity must have been understood before the structure of the solar system, because it is a basic principle of classical celestial mechanics. The actual history of astronomy is the reverse—Copernicus and Kepler came before Newton. Probably Greek historians of mathematics had little idea of its earliest stages and simply attached their axiomatic presuppositions to the well-known name of Thales.

But the legends have their own interest. On the one hand they suggest a kind of interpretative error to be avoided in trying to understand the history of mathematics. On the other hand, the Thales legends provide a very nice example of the Greek image of the mathematician. Thales was a man who understood all branches of knowledge, for wisdom is not naturally fragmented. All wisdom was a whole; philosophy and mathematics were part of the same truth. Thales could be successful in a practical way, but he preferred speculative thought. His detachment is related in an anecdote with which most Greeks are familiar: while walking along one evening looking up at the stars, Thales is supposed to have fallen into a ditch, drawing the comment from his attendant, "How can you know what is doing in the heavens if you cannot see what is at your feet?"

In the half century following Thales, until its final tragic destruction by the Persians in 494 B.C., Miletus was the intellectual center of the Greek world. Thales' student Anaximander was more a philosopher-astronomer than a mathematician. Anaximander evolved a theory of opposites that was to dominate Greek thought about the natural world. We sense the world as a set of oppositions, according to Anaximander, and the most basic opposites are hot and cold, wet and dry. Thales had oversimplified in calling water, the wet, primary; it was better to talk of the opposites separating out of an infinite, boundless, primal substance. For a substance to encroach on its opposite was an "injustice"—the separation of opposites is the characteristic feature of the present world.

Anaximander's world view was in agreement with this philosophy: the earth was shaped like a short cylinder, one-third as deep as the diameter of either base. It was suspended in the middle of the universe and needed no support, since it was equidistant from all the extremities. The stars and planets, the moon, and the sun were on concentric rings outside the earth; the diameter of the moon's ring was nineteen times the earth's, and the sun's was twenty-seven or twenty-eight times the earth's. Anaximander is also supposed to have introduced the gnomon into Greek astronomy—like Thales, he traveled to Babylon and Egypt—and Herodotus says he drew an early map of the world.

If anything, Pythagoras is the most elusive figure among the three Ionians. But his name is the best known, principally because it is attached to that right triangle property. Pythagoras, according to legend, studied with Anaximander and may also have lived in Egypt and Babylonia for several years. Pythagoras is said to have emigrated from the island of Samos to Crotone, in southern Italy, to escape the despotic rule of Polycrates. He may not have been a real person at all, but rather, a composite of those who belonged to a mystical brotherhood that emerged in Crotone. Apparently, the members of the society attributed their discoveries to the Master, and it is of such stuff that legends are made.

You can sum up Pythagorean doctrine with "all is number." Mathematicians and historians of mathematics are inclined to write off this number mysticism. But I am convinced that some of the ideas of the Pythagoreans contributed to important discoveries in mathematics and related areas, and, even if they hadn't, they are part of the mathematical tradition of the West.

The Pythagoreans made important discoveries that, for them, verified this philosophy of number. They found, for example, a way of explaining harmony in music. If two harp strings were of the same thickness and under the same tension, the strings would produce the musical interval of an octave if the ratio of their lengths was 2:1. Length ratios of 3:2 and 4:3 produced the fifth and the fourth, and a ratio of 9:8 gave a relationship that modern music does not recognize—the Greeks called it a "tone."

From this idea that small-number ratios could harmonize, the Pythagoreans drew an almost endless number of conclusions.

They worked out, to begin with, a theory of means. The first three means were the arithmetic, the geometric, and the harmonic:

> Arithmetic: the first number exceeds the second by the same amount as the second exceeds the third.
> Geometric: the first number is to the second as the second is to the third.
> Harmonic: by whatever part of itself the first exceeds the second, the second exceeds the third by the same part of the third.

For example:

> 5 is the arithmetic mean of 2 and 8;
> 4 is the geometric mean of 2 and 8;
> $\frac{16}{5}$ is the harmonic mean of 2 and 8;

(since its reciprocal, $\frac{5}{16}$, is the arithmetic mean of the reciprocals of 2 and 8).

The Pythagoreans found several important associations for the geometric mean, including that of the construction of the pentagram, the emblem of their society. This involved the golden section, which in turn brought out all kinds of fanciful theories, including that of the proportions of the pyramids, which I mentioned earlier.

The theory of means allowed the Pythagoreans to make a modification of Anaximander's philosophy. Rather than the merging of opposites being an "injustice," the opposites that make up the universe could be harmonized by the mean. A blend of opposites was possible; the essence of opposites was not their separation.

The Pythagoreans applied this new philosophy widely. The goal of medicine, for instance, was to blend the opposites hot-cold and wet-dry in the human body. A predominance of any

Raphael's Pythagoras *may be somewhat romanticized, since some historians question whether or not Pythagoras was an individual, rather than something of a composite figure. Real or legendary, individual or composite, Pythagoras has had substantial impact in philosophy, music, and mathematics.*

one would produce sickness. Music did the same thing for the soul that medicine did for the body—it purified it by harmony.

In astronomy, the Pythagoreans may have been the first to suggest that the earth was spherical in shape. Pythagoras seems to have proposed the idea that each planet had a different speed, producing a different musical note—later Pythagoreans claimed that Pythagoras was so pure that he could actually hear the "harmony of the spheres." Philolaus, one of the few early Pythagoreans whose work has survived even in fragments, believed that the earth was too gross to have the position at the center of the universe. He suggested that the earth, the moon, the sun, the five planets and the sphere of the stars revolved around a central fire—the first nonearth-centered cosmology in world history. The part of the earth where Greece lay was always turned away from the central fire, while the anti-earth, the *antichthon*, made the central fire invisible to people on the other side of the earth as well. The anti-earth stayed between the earth and the central fire, permanently eclipsing it.

Aristotle made a few ironic remarks about this astronomical system:

> When the Pythagoreans anywhere find a gap in the numerical ratios of things, they fill it up in order to complete the system. As ten is the perfect number (because it is the sum of the first four numbers) they maintain that there must be ten bodies moving in the universe, and as only nine are visible they make the antichthon the tenth.

There is some justice to Aristotle's criticism, for the Pythagoreans did not always confirm their theories by observation with quite the rigor they had used in investigating musical chords. But any scientist has a tendency to make the world fit his model of it, especially when the model is as beautiful as the Pythagoreans'. Starting with an interest in numbers, the Pythagoreans had worked out a comprehensive world view in a way comparable to the Zuñi Indians with their fours and sixes, and to the philosopher Kant when he asserted that mathematical truths are *a priori* independent of and prior to experience and experiment.

The Pythagorean interest in numbers produced some good mathematics as well. Pythagoras and his students probably developed or experimented with early stages of the axiomatic method in geometry. Eudemus, a pupil of Aristotle, says that the Pythagoreans discovered that the sum of the angles of any triangle is equal to two right angles (i.e., equals 180°). The proof was essentially the same as in modern geometry texts.

And it is likely that Pythagoreans knew and studied most of the five "Platonic" solids. Philolaus called the cube a "geometric harmony," because it had twelve edges, three angles, and six faces, and eight was the harmonic mean of six and twelve.

The best-known mathematical discovery of the school, however, was the "Pythagorean theorem." The Babylonians knew and used the right triangle property long before Pythagoras, and Pythagoras may have learned it, as a technique, when he visited Babylonia. But apparently the Babylonians had nothing like a general proof for the theorem, while Pythagoras himself may have been capable of an axiomatic demonstration.

Dabbling with either the geometric mean of the right triangle proposition could have led the Pythagoreans to a horrendous discovery. There are numbers, and in particular, the square root of 2, which cannot be represented as the ratio of one whole number to another. These are the numbers that are now called "irrationals," and much ado is made of them these days.

The discovery must have created quite a stir in academic circles, and legend has it that one Hippasus, a society member who let out the secret, was drowned for his indiscretion. Discovery of these "incommensurables" did create a logical scandal in terms of Pythagorean philosophy, which held that number, the basic way of understanding the world, was made up of units in isolation from one another.

The Pythagoreans found a way of approximating the square root of 2 as closely as they wanted—as apparently had the Babylonians before them. But, no matter how close they came, 2 always lay between their upper and lower approximations.

In the fifth century B.C., the Pythagorean society had

The temple of Poseidon, in Italy, has survived in much better condition than has most of the architecture of the period.

considerable political influence in southern Italy. Pythagoras reached a powerful position in Crotone, but for some reason he was driven out toward the end of his life by a reaction of the aristocrats, and he died in Metapontum.

Parmenides, a philosopher born about 515 B.C., made the neighboring city of Elea an intellectual center. Parmenides held that space was a full, continuous, indivisible whole, a view directly opposed to the Pythagoreans' view of a discontinuous reality. His argument was involved, but it was based on the central proposition that anything that can be thought of must exist. This is like asserting that a vacuum is not nothing, since we can conceive of it and name it—a vacuum is a thing, even if it is scientifically defined as a space devoid of matter.

Parmenides' pupil Zeno put the dilemma of the continuous versus the discontinuous into a set of four mathematical paradoxes, which apparently left the great thinkers of his time a bit shaken. The paradoxes showed that, in terms of the Pythagorean tradition of thought, motion is not possible. Here are three of the paradoxes, the fourth, stadium, is ambiguous:

I. *Dichotomy:*

An object cannot move from one point to another. For to move from point 1 to point 8, the object must first move halfway, to 4. Before it can move to 4, it must move half of that distance, to 2. Before 2, 1, and so on *ad infinitum*. Therefore the object can never start to move.

II. Achilles:

If Achilles and a tortoise start a race, with Achilles a certain distance behind the tortoise, Achilles can never overtake the tortoise. For in the time Achilles has reached the point where the tortoise started, the tortoise will have advanced to a new point. When Achilles reaches the new point, the tortoise will have advanced to yet another point. And so on, ad infinitum.

III. An arrow, shot through the air, cannot move. For at any instant it is in a certain position; it is at rest. Since time is composed of an infinite number of instants, the arrow is always at rest.

Zeno meant his paradoxes to support Parmenides' philosophy that the world is indivisible, that there can be neither a multiplicity of things nor motion. But the mathematical implications of the paradoxes have been more important. Their mathematical source was not fully understood until the eighteenth century, well after the development of the calculus.

In its early history, Greek thought had centered in Ionia. Pythagoras' emigration had shifted the intellectual focus to southern Italy. Around 459 B.C., Parmenides and Zeno traveled to Athens, and for the next century or so Athens was to be the center of learning in the Greek world. Parmenides met Socrates, a young man at that time, and Zeno argued his paradoxes dialectically to the Athenians. Seventy-five years later, Plato was to write a dialogue called "Parmenides," in which that philosopher argues his anti-Pythagorean view. And Plato remembers the visit when he introduces in two other dialogues an "Eleatic stranger."

With its naval defeat of the Persians in 479 B.C., Athens had begun its cultural efflorescence—the "Age of Pericles." Its democratic political form resulted partly from its class structure, which was in turn a reflection of Athens' status as a sea power. Inland Sparta could maintain an oligarchy depending on a tremendous slave population, the Helots, because the agricultural economy and the army were managed by an elite. Athens, on the other hand, depended on its urban poor to man the navy, and on a large commercial class which was quite articulate in demanding political rights.

Athens' rivalry with Sparta soon developed into the disastrous Peloponnesian War (431–404 B.C.), which exhausted the resources of mainland Greece and ended all prospects of Greece's becoming politically united without outside domination. But as long as Athens remained free and a democracy of sorts, the political turbulence and dynamism of the city seemed to be a stimulant to Greek thought.

The correlation between democracy and intellectual creativity, however, is not completely straightforward. In 399 B.C., Socrates was condemned to death for impiety and for corrupting the Athenian youth. He was a stonemason's son who had become the most influential philosopher in Greece. The charge really meant, it seems, that Socrates' judges considered him too sympathetic to the aristocracy, for he had criticized the composition of the Athenian assembly and the ignorance of Athenian officials. And some of Socrates' students had been notoriously anti-democratic—Alcibiades and Critias, for example, who planned oligarchical revolutions in 411 and 404 B.C. Socrates' student and successor as Athens' foremost thinker, Plato, had similar aristocratic leanings: his ideal state, set out in *The Republic*, had little in common with the Athenian democracy.

After the death of Socrates, Plato traveled to southern Italy, where he was befriended by Archytas of Tarentum, perhaps the most remarkable of the later Pythagoreans. Archytas was accomplished in almost everything that the Greeks admired. He was the unbeaten general of his city-state's army for seven years, and seems to have saved Plato from death at the hands of Dionysius, the unscrupulous tyrant of Syracuse. Most of Archytas' writings are lost, but he is supposed to have believed in a universe of infinite extent. "If I were at the outside [of the universe]," a later writer quotes him, "could I stretch my hand or stick outwards or not? To suppose that I could not is absurd." Archytas also wrote a mathematical treatise on mechanics, an axiomatic study of geometry, a work on musical chords, and a proof that there is not a rational geometric mean between any number n and its successor, n+1. And he is reputed to have constructed a mechanical dove, of wood, which actually flew.

When Plato returned to Athens, he founded his Academy, the first real university in ancient history—a communal society with its own chapel, modeled on the Pythagorean society. It endured until 529 A.D. Over the entrance of the original Academy were the words, "Let no one destitute of geometry enter my doors."

Plato's great influence in mathematics did not come from any original contributions of his own, but from his enthusiasm for mathematics as training for the mind. He objected to words in Greek geometric terminology like "squaring," "applying," "adding," and "producing," because they implied that the object of geometry was practical. The true purpose of geometry was knowledge. A circle drawn with a compass was an approximation, a perishable object; the eternal and true circle was the idea of the circle, the ideal circle. And this relation between the abstract and the real in mathematics was Plato's perfect illustration for his philosophy: as the ideal properties of the circle were more important than the actual circle, so also the ideal object, the ideal chair, the ideal straight line, the ideal good, the ideal beautiful were the essence of philosophy.

Plato often used mathematical illustrations in his philosophy. In "Timaeus," a dialogue with a Pythagorean speaker, Plato deals with the five regular solids—hereafter in Greek thought called the "Platonic solids." He built the solids up by combining plane figures, equating the first four with the four elements of Greek natural philosophy:

tetrahedron	fire	hot and dry
octahedron	air	hot and moist
icosahedron	water	cold and moist
cube	earth	cold and dry

Confronted, then, with the fifth solid—the dodecahedron—Plato decided that it should represent the universe itself.

Plato divided mathematics into four branches: arithmetic (which had more the meaning of number theory than of basic calculations), geometry, solid geometry, and astronomy. His conception of astronomy has been the most difficult to understand. For him, the motions of the celestial bodies were as approximate to true astronomy as the drawn circle was to the true circle. In *The Republic*, Plato suggests that the astronomer does not even have to look at the heavens. Plato has been condemned for this extreme idealist position, but to hold him responsible for the eventual stagnation of Greek science, as some historians of science have done, is an exaggeration. As no Greek city-state immediately adopted the constitution of *The Republic*, so later Greek scientists were in practice critical of Plato's advice to minimize observations. Eudoxus, for example, the most brilliant young mathematician attracted to the Academy, said that, rather than guessing about the nature of the sun, he would not mind being burned up if that were the price of getting close to the sun and observing it.

Eudoxus' writings, like those of all other Greek mathematicians before Euclid, have been lost. But most of the later commentators, including Euclid himself, credit Eudoxus with a mathematical answer to the Pythagorean discovery of incommensurables and to Zeno's paradoxes—an answer that made Euclid's work possible. Eudoxus invented the method of *exhaustion*, which anticipated the concept of the limit in modern calculus. Exhaustion was a technique based on the principle that, contrary to the Pythagoreans' view, a mathematician does not have to assume the existence of an infinitely small magnitude. All that is necessary is that he be able, by continual division, to make a magnitude as small as he wishes.

Eudoxus made important contributions to astronomy as well as to mathematics. He showed that the peculiar motions of a planet could be explained by the motion of four spheres concentric to the earth. This model was a precursor to Ptolemy's classical theory of epicycles, the type of explanation that endured until Copernicus. And Eudoxus apparently knew a good deal about the length of the year, again ignoring Plato's advice; for example, he was the first Greek to suggest a calendar of three 365-day years alternating with one 366-day year.

One manifestation of Plato's idealism in mathematics was his insistence that geometric constructions be made with compass (and his was of the collapsible variety) and straightedge. This dictum was accepted for some thousands of years.

Greek mathematicians and their successors down through the nineteenth century were particularly frustrated in their efforts to solve three problems under Plato's restrictions. These three, which have become known as the "Classical Problems of Antiquity," are:

1. Duplication of a cube—to construct a cube having volume double that of a given cube;
2. Trisection of an angle—to divide any angle into three equal parts;
3. Quadrature of the circle—to construct a square with area that of a given circle.

The problems have been solved in many ways—Archytas was among those who came up with solutions—but not under Plato's rules. But it was not until the nineteenth century A.D. that mathematicians proved that the problems could not be solved with compass and straightedge. In the meantime, there was much good mathematical spin-off from the assaults on the problems.

8

MATHEMATICAL ROADS
LEAD TO ALEXANDRIA

Alexander the Great planned a city to be built in an ideal location, not far from the westernmost mouth of the Nile, in a spot sheltered by the island of Pharos. There is a narrow limestone ridge along the coast, and a supply of fresh water from inland Lake Mareotis, which would eventually provide a link, via canals, with the Nile itself and from there to the eastern seas.

Alexander did not live to see his city even begun, but the project was handled most capably by Ptolemy, one of his generals. The city was carefully planned and constructed with broad avenues lined with columns, trees, and marble buildings. There were Greek statues and Egyptian obelisks in great number, temples to the various gods and goddesses, along with synagogues, for the Jews outnumbered the Greeks in the city. The largest of the temples was that of Serapis, the city's principal deity, who combined the qualities of an ancient Egyptian god with those of a Greek counterpart. There were also bazaars, theaters, baths, market places, a race course, and a gymnasium, all done on a grand scale.

But the pride of that first Ptolemy and his successors—the dynasty ruled Alexandria for about three hundred years—was the Museum and the Library. By 200 B.C. Alexandria was the intellectual center of the Western world, and the Library contained about 500,000 volumes or, more accurately, rolls, which were being carefully catalogued and copied by a force of scribes and artists. Sea captains who sailed from Alexandria to all parts of the Mediterranean area, the Indian Ocean, and probably even to China, were commissioned to bring back books. In fact, anyone bringing a book to Alexandria was required by law to submit it to the Library, that the scholars might check it against their holdings and, if it proved to be new, copy it.

The first Ptolemy lured scholars—poets, philosophers, grammarians, mathematicians, astronomers, geographers, physicians, historians—to Alexandria with promises of free room, board, and whatever else they needed for a comfortable life. One of the first to come was the mathematician Euclid.

Now I suspect that, if I were emphasizing mathematics rather than history, this would be the time to speak at length and glowingly about the *Elements* of Euclid. Certainly his works, which consisted of the systematic organization of the mathematical results to his time, have been highly regarded to the present. And "geometry" for most people means "Euclidean geometry." But I am quite sure that Euclid's efforts had relatively little impact on the average citizen of his time, and may not even have been considered terribly important by his colleagues at the Museum.

One of his students, Archimedes, did become famous in his own time, and, when Archimedes left the cloistered life of the Museum for a more active participation in Syracuse, he wrote to the scholars back in Alexandria. Much of what is known about Archimedes and his work is known through this correspondence.

Archimedes is often ranked as one of the three greatest mathematicians of all history. (The other two usually mentioned are Newton and Gauss.) Archimedes attained legendary status even in his own time and was respected by scholar and king alike. I suspect that the rulers, in particular Hiero of Syra-

The Roman soldiers interrupt Archimedes as he muses upon matters geometrical. Have you ever wondered how credible is this report of the death of Archimedes, considering the age of the tale and the propensity, on the part of many scholars, to glorify the Greeks and denigrate the Romans?

cuse, were more impressed by the mechanical genius of Archimedes than with his mathematical accomplishments. One legend has it that he did the king a considerable service by determining that a goldsmith was cheating him by introducing a base metal into a supposedly pure gold crown. (And, in the process, Archimedes is said to have dashed out of his bath, where he had his inspiration, and down the street shouting, "Eureka, eureka.")

Archimedes also helped prolong the siege of Syracuse by the Romans through the invention of some very effective devices of war. But he himself is said to have thought more of his accomplishments in pure mathematics than he did of these applications. In his attacks on mathematical problems Archimedes showed greater imagination and freedom of action than had many of his predecessors and contemporaries, who were hindered often by too serious consideration of purely geometrical methods. Archimedes used his mechanical devices and investigations to further his purely mathematical work.

In some of his work on finding areas of regions bounded by curved lines, Archimedes anticipated the invention of the calculus nearly two thousand years later. He also worked on problems that are now considered part of the differential calculus. He determined a quite accurate value for the ratio of the circumference to the diameter of a circle.

An account by Plutarch has it that Archimedes died under the sword of a Roman soldier when Syracuse finally fell. The incident makes a good story and certainly helps to enhance the reputation of the Romans as the antithesis of the Greeks in their disregard for scholarly interests.

One of those with whom Archimedes corresponded was Eratosthenes, possibly the most versatile scholar of his time—poet, philosopher, historian, chronologist, geographer, as well as mathematician. Unfortunately, Eratosthenes' mathematical work is lost, except for that familiar "sieve" for locating prime numbers. He was called to Alexandria originally to direct the Library, and was regarded in his own time as a second Plato.

He took a world view of geography, of which there is evidence in his world map. Apparently he was a tireless collector of data from travelers, traders, and others who made Alexandria one of their regular stops. Eratosthenes' best-known feat is his computation of the size of the earth. By using two angles of the sun's position from two cities, and a fairly accurate reckoning of the distance between the cities, he apparently determined that the earth was close to 25,000 miles in circumference

This "portrait" of Aristotle was done by Raphael, and I suspect the artist may have used some artistic license. On the other hand, this may meet your criteria of how Aristotle should have appeared. Courtesy Scripta Mathematica.

—quite a remarkable result, if indeed the interpretations are accurate. Not so incidentally, one of the implications of this result is that Eratosthenes knew the earth to be spherical—a view probably held by most educated men of his era and, in fact, of subsequent eras.

Some of the Greek astronomers believed the sun to be the center of the solar system, and suggested that the earth revolved around the sun. This theory was advanced in particular by Aristarchus of Samos, contrary view of the better known Aristotle and Ptolemy notwithstanding.

The mathematicians of this "first" Alexandrian era were also astronomers—perhaps even primarily astronomers. Among these was Apollonius of Perga, who may have been born about the time Eratosthenes died. Apollonius' great work dealt with the conic sections—those curves derived from slicing a cone. His efforts were not surpassed until the seventeenth century at the earliest, and he was known in his own time as the Great Geometer. Apollonius died about 190 B.C., and his death marks the end of the period of cultural flourishing at Alexandria. Some argue that Apollonius was indeed the last great "Greek" mathematician, that such as Diophantus, Pappus, Heron, and others of the second and third centuries of the Christian era were not significant. And this, it seems to me, is a debatable point of view. Whatever your inclination on this, Alexandria did experience a decline of some centuries following the time of Apollonius.

Actually, the scholarly life at the Museum and Library went on at its usual leisurely pace, though there were apparently few if any outstanding scholars, other than Hipparchus, in. the two and a half centuries after the time of Apollonius. Hipparchus was perhaps the greatest astronomer of antiquity, who combined theoretical insight, discovery, and interpretation with the practical invention of astronomical instruments.

Outside the cloistered walls, there was little tranquillity. The fourth ruler in the Ptolemaic dynasty was a depraved individual whose reign was characterized by decadence and debauchery at best, with occasional violence, including the elimination of real and imagined rivals to his throne. The decline continued throughout the reigns of his successors.

And, with the royalty setting the pace, the rank and file of Alexandria followed the lead. The population of the city was quite a mixture—a potentially explosive mixture, at that. For, while Alexandria was nominally a Greek city, the Egyptians far outnumbered the Greeks, and their numbers were matched approximately by those of the Jews. The Greeks constituted the nobility—the leisure class—and controlled most of the money, hence the political power in the city. As the strength of the rulers declined, that of the wealthy Greeks increased. And, as the rich became richer, the poor became poorer.

It is always dangerous to generalize on the characteristics and behavior of a population. But reports of contemporaries in other parts of the world suggest that the "typical" Alexandrian was something less than a model citizen. In fact, the term "Alexandrian" was synonymous at the time with "rascal." He was not exactly slothful but was inclined, given the choice, toward socializing rather than hard work. With the nobles setting the pace, the social climate deteriorated substantially, until the scholars began to be affected. The ensuing exodus and decline of the academic center continued until the middle of the first century B.C., when the Cleopatra of whom Shakespeare wrote so much reversed the trend—and this despite her own rather shabby reputation.

Many mathematics commentators these days tend to glorify Greek mathematical accomplishments and deprecate those of the Egyptians and Romans. And, I'll grant that the Greek mathematical achievements were substantial. But, to be consistent with the idea of writing off the Egyptians, should these commentators not also write off the Greek geometry, since, with the invention of projective geometry, in particular, men such as Pascal and Descartes were able to generalize in a few theorems what the Greeks took dozens, even hundreds, of theorems and corollaries to say?

And, too, the evaluation of much Greek mathematics and the accomplishments of Greek mathematicians depends upon the observations of writers who lived much later than did the mathematicians. Take, as an example, Eudoxus, who is very well thought of in mathematics circles and is sometimes described as having anticipated the ideas of such men as Cantor and Dedekind, whose work is considered to be the very foundation of "modern" mathematics. Nothing remains of the mathematical work of Eudoxus, and he is known only through writings of Proculus (who was not a mathematician) some ten centuries after the time of Eudoxus.

On the other hand, the geometry of such men as Menelaus and Pappus seems more in keeping with the ideas of Pascal and Desargues, though here again most of the original writing has been lost. But Pappus and Menelaus are of another era— the "second Alexandrian era"—and that is another story.

9

SCIENCE AND TECHNOLOGY

While Alexandria was rising and then declining as a center of culture, what was happening back in Greece? That rocky peninsula of the Athenians and Spartans was well removed from the Greek centers such as Alexandria, but it was the original source of Greek culture, the language, the philosophy, the literature, and even the mathematics (though if you count them up, you may suspect that Greek mathematicians come from anyplace but Greece).

It was during this Alexandrian period that an upstart people of the Italian peninsula were making themselves known around the Mediterranean. After they had conquered most of the peninsula, these Romans turned to such sites as Carthage, Syracuse (where posterity has given them a black mark for allegedly killing Archimedes), and Greece. They conquered Greece with ease. This conquest resulted in a blending of the two cultures with rather remarkable results.

Many people are inclined to say that this blending was a one-sided affair, that the Romans were an uncultured people disinclined toward intellectual matters, and, in particular, not interested in mathematics at all. Or only interested in rule-of-thumb solutions, rather than elegant geometric theorems. On the other hand, the Greeks brought to this blending centuries of literature and philosophical thought and a long tradition of

The Romans are usually written off as contributing nothing to the development of mathematics. But they did use the practical mathematics of their predecessors in their architecture, surveying, cartography, and other applications. And I would hazard the conjecture that their approximations and rules of thumb, developed in these areas, led to their mathematizing, perhaps by the "Greeks" at Alexandria. This is something of a romanticization of Vespasian planning the Coliseum.

mathematics. What Rome did bring to this meeting of two cultures were a vigor of a people on the move and some substantial problems related to the ordering of an expanding empire.

There were the very practical considerations of waging wars of conquest (and one should remember that the great spread of Greek culture came in the wake of the conquests of Alexander the Great). Waging war successfully and on a large scale called for the development of weapons and machines.

Having conquered the area, the Romans needed to be concerned with the administration of government and provision of public services. In particular, there was the matter of water supply and problems of transportation and communication. These were urgent practical matters. And, while such problems involved, and have always involved, some mathematics, the considerations were not the sort to inspire extension of the mathematics of the Greeks.

On the other hand, you can hardly write the Romans off as completely practical or anti-intellectual, as some imply. Many of the noble class admired the Greek literature and language and learned the speech of the conquered people. For such citizens—and these were the men who governed Rome and the provinces—this was a bilingual period. They were even encouraged by the poet Ovid to master both Latin and Greek in order that they would not bore the ladies in their lives. Neither Ovid nor anyone else is recorded as having said anything about doing mathematics in both languages, but, I suspect that the educated Roman, or the Roman with an inclination toward mathematics, did study Euclid, Apollonius, and the other great mathematicians in Greek. Much ado has been made over the fact that Euclid's *Elements* were not translated into Latin until well into the Christian era long after the Greco-Roman period. But in that era there was little need for a translation. The educated citizen read Greek. The practical man didn't need to have proved to him that when a line cuts a pair of parallel lines equal angles are formed.

Having thus relegated mathematics to the role of a gentleman's indoor sport for this era, I propose to turn briefly to the sciences. What was the significance of Greek and Roman science in the development of the technology needed for the solution of the practical problems? What, if any, was the "spin-off" from these practical considerations for the development of a Roman science?

One of the greatest of the Alexandrian scientists was Strato, apparently lived the early part of the third century B.C. Practically nothing is known of Strato himself or his own writings, but much of what he wrote and many of his ideas were preserved by the better-known Hero (sometimes Heron) of Alexandria, who wrote probably in the first century of the Christian era.

Strato was inclined toward an experimental approach in science, as indeed was Hero, and the following short passage, attributed to Strato, shows how he sized up two different approaches to science:

> The science of pneumatics was held in high regard of old by philosophers and engineers, the former logically deducing its principles, the latter determining them by experimental tests. What we have felt constrained to do in this book is to give an orderly exposition of the established principles of the science and add thereto our own discoveries. We hope in this way to be of service to future students of the subject.

He then led off with a rather remarkable discussion of the nature of the vacuum. It is interesting to note that the two views on science then are still in evidence—the philosopher of Strato's time is succeeded by the theoretical physicist and pure mathematician of our time, who profess to disdain the cookbook methods of the engineer. The engineer retaliates with scorn for the ivory tower theorizing of the others. And from their varied efforts came progress in both technology and theory.

Apparently, though, the Greek passion for logical consistency—a mathematical system—did weaken their science. Archimedes, for example, is said to have cared little for his practical results and mechanical innovations compared to his work in "pure" mathematics.

Then, too, there was little need in the Greek civilization for the application of science to such matters as laborsaving devices. There were ample slaves to do the work. Why build machines?

Hero reports that scientific know-how was applied as a handmaiden to religion in the generation and fabrication of miracles. The principle of the siphon was employed in a device that apparently turned water into wine. The study of optics—and this was a favorite among the Greeks, including Euclid, who wrote a book on the topic—was applied to the production of apparitions. Magnets were used in various and imaginative ways, as were improved methods of lighting. As a background, to lend sound effects to amplify the effect of these other phenomena, Hero reports the use of organ music.

Both the siphon and the organ are applications of Strato's science of pneumatics. Another manifestation of the same science—the expansive power of hot air—was also used to enhance the mystery of religion. Hero reports that in some shrines an air chamber in the altar was connected to a small chamber housing a statue of the deity. When the offering was burned on the altar, the expanding hot air was conveyed to the chamber, opening the door and moving the statue forward toward the worshiper, a process that must have been quite impressive to the average citizen of the time.

Ctesibius, who was a contemporary of Strato, contributed such practical devices as a water clock, a water organ—whose tones impressed Cicero some two centuries later—and a fire engine, which has been called his "masterpiece."

The water clock was remarkable in that it accounted for

the seasonal variation in the length of the day. Day and night were each divided into twelve equal intervals. Thus, there were more daylight hours in the summer and fewer in the winter.

The contributions of such experimental scientists as Strato and Ctesibius are representative of the tradition (however weak) that the Romans met and absorbed as they extended their political power throughout the Greek world. There is no clear-cut evidence of how the tradition was continued or changed by the Romans, but they were less inclined toward religious effects and, as I noted, more concerned wtih some major practical problems.

One of these problems was that of maintaining an adequate supply of pure water for the city of Rome, in particular, and also for the other cities. On this there is a carefully detailed account by Sextus Julius Frontinus, who was appointed the equivalent of water commissioner by Emperor Nerva about the year 100. Frontinus apparently familiarized himself with every facet of the water supply system in order, he notes, to be sure that his subordinates were really doing their jobs. His account, *De Aquis*, contains a mass of data on costs, amount of water needed, and details involved in the construction of aqueducts.

Frontinus describes how certain illegal pipes were built into some of the aqueducts to draw off water for private purposes (though he points out that the alertness of the water department led to the discovery and destruction of these), and he mentions other frauds that were attempted. But, all in all, he was quite pleased with the water supply system and notes: "With such an array of indispensable structures carrying so many waters compare, if you will, the idle pyramids or the useless though famous works of the Greeks."

Frontinus did have a strong feeling for the benefits of this application of science. One of his statements seems particularly appropriate today.

"The effect of this care displayed by the Emperor Nerva,

most public-spirited of rulers, is felt from day to day increasingly and will be still more felt in the health of the city. . . . Not even the waste water is lost. The appearance of the city is clean and altered. The air is purer, and the causes of the unwholesome atmosphere which gave the city so bad a name with earlier generations are now removed."

In architecture, the Romans were strongly influenced by the Greeks both technically and aesthetically. In the latter half of the first century B.C., when Rome was in a dynamic period of rebuilding under the first emperor Augustus, Vitruvius wrote his *De Architectura*, a manual of Roman knowledge. "Architecture" for Vitruvius encompassed much more than it does in its modern definition: city planning, the design and construction of temples, public buildings and private houses, interior decoration, water supply, sundials and clocks, and some practical mechanics. The broad definition of the subject was probably a reflection of Vitruvius' own experience: although he had been trained in building techniques, Vitruvius served the emperor by managing the army's war machines (the ballistae and scorpions) and later by maintaining the plumbing system of Rome. Roman scientists seem to have been all-round technical handymen.

The Romans made a number of architectural innovations. They invented concrete, which enabled them to build much larger structures than the Greeks had done. The Greeks did not begin to use the arch until late Roman times. But the Romans developed it much earlier, together with the closely related vaulted dome, so that ceilings and spans could go unsupported for much greater distances than in Greek architecture. The Pantheon in Rome, for example, built in 27 B.C. and still standing, has a circular rotunda 140 feet high and 140 feet across.

The Romans have left no record of the techniques they used for laying out the curve of an arch—the common semicircular arch would not have been difficult. We are fairly sure that nothing like the mathematical calculations of stress found in modern engineering existed in Roman architecture. The Romans probably discovered the strength of an arch and its buttresses by trial and error; and the fact that so many Roman buildings have survived for two thousand years suggests that they were built much stronger than was necessary for their immediate purposes. In other words, since the Romans had no way of determining the precise strength of their constructions, they generally made them as strong as possible, just to be safe. Vitruvius' only theoretical advice on arches was that their stones be wedge-shaped, with the joints all pointing toward the center, and that if the buttresses "are of wide dimensions, they will restrain the thrust and give stability to the buildings." Vitruvius' application of mathematics to building layout is based on a Pythagorean concept of numerical symmetry and proportion: "Without symmetry and proportion," he says, "no temple can have a regular plan; that is, it must have an exact proportion worked out after the fashion of a finely-shaped human body." One perfect number, Vitruvius tells us, is 10— a reference to Pythagorean theory—and 10 is not only the sum of the first four integers, but it is the number of the fingers. And 6 is another perfect number (by Pythagorean theory, because it is the sum of its factors: $6=1+2+3$); it is the ratio between a man's height and the length of his foot. Vitruvius expands with an elaborate discussion of how 6 and its proportions can be used architecturally.

Vitruvius' work was intended, by his own admission, as a practical manual written for the foreman and the "works manager." For such practical readers he notes such a matter as that of preparation of seasoned timber: "In felling a tree cut the trunk into the very heart and leave it standing so that the sap may drain completely out. This lets the useless liquid run out through the sapwood and the quality of the wood will not be corrupted. Then, and not till then, let the tree be felled and it will be in the highest state of usefulness."

He also perpetuates a strange notion that northern people have deep voices and southern people have shrill voices, and imparts some totally erroneous theories about winds.

All in all, though, *De Architectura* is a monumental work, a peerless source of information about Roman science, technology, and even fresco painting.

Posidonius, who established a school in Rhodes in the first century B.C., worked at quantifying natural phenomena, in particular the measurement of tides and other matters of geography. Posidonius was rated a competent mathematician by Proculus, that comprehensive commentator of the fifth century, and, apparently he did have some substantial influence in other matters as well.

His measurement of the circumference of the earth was well off that optimum figure attributed to Eratosthenes (though keep in mind that the latter's best figure is reckoned on the basis of one interpretation of the unit of measure) and was accepted by Ptolemy, the great astronomer and geographer of the early Christian era. Ptolemy's data were generally accepted throughout the Western world for many centuries and are said to have been used by Christopher Columbus.

Geminus, a protégé of Posidonius, wrote an extensive commentary on the science of the time. His attempts to quantify natural phenomena were, I suspect, rather typical of the time and reflect, among other things, the conviction that heavenly bodies move in circles. This conviction, which dates to the Pythagoreans, led the ancient astronomers to develop some elaborate theories to account for things they observed. The most famous of these theories is that of Ptolemy's epicycles, but before remarking on that, I'll mention a simpler matter expounded by Geminus.

The astronomers noted that the four seasons of the year

were not of equal length. From the spring equinox to the summer tropic 94½ days elapsed. The time from the summer tropic to the autumn equinox was 92½ days; from the autumn equinox to the winter tropic, 88⅛ days; and, from the winter tropic to the spring equinox, 90⅛ days. But, they were convinced that the sun's rate of speed was the same throughout the year (and, just possibly, Aristarchus had some lasting influence after all). So, if the sun's path were a circle, how could they account for these seasonal differences in the time it took for the sun to travel a quarter of the circle?

Geminus resolves the problem as follows: "But in fact the sun moves not only on a lower but on an eccentric circle, as the accompanying figure shows. The center of the circle is not the same as that of the zodiacal circle, but is thrust to one side. On account of this position the course of the sun is divided into four unequal parts." The explanation was not appreciably improved upon for quite a few centuries, and, when it comes right down to it, the argument could probably suffice for most people today. The big hurdle was the conviction that things traveled in circles. The inequality of the seasons could be explained quite simply if the ellipse path were accepted, but the ellipse lacked the mathematical purity of the circle.

Claudius Ptolemy followed Geminus and Posidonius by more than two centuries, and he greatly elaborated upon their simple geometric explanations. Ptolemy gives much credit for ideas contained in his great work (which we know by the Arab name *Almagest*) to Hipparchus. Hipparchus apparently studied and observed at Rhodes in the second century B.C., but none of his writings have survived.

Ptolemy is remembered more for his erroneous interpretation of the nature of the solar system than for his more original contributions in the area of mathematical geography and cartography. His theories in this area were based upon a very complicated system of circles and provided for an explanation of things that the simple heliocentric system proposed by Aristarchus did not.

I will not attempt to explain the Ptolemaic system of epicycles in detail. Imagine the relative positions of sun, earth, and the planet Venus, which will give you an insight into why such a wrong theory survived unchallenged for so long.

Most obviously, the sun appears to move. And traditionally, the ancients placed themselves at the center of their respective world pictures, from the "middle place" of the Zuñi to the "Middle Kingdom" of the Chinese. The earth-centered model agreed with the Greek ideas of physics. The earth had to be stationary, according to Ptolemy, for if it moved "the solid bodies on it would always appear to have been left behind in the motion of the earth."

Also, there were at least two observations that a simple heliocentric did not explain: the inequality of the seasons, and the lack of stellar parallax.

The first of these can be explained by "off-centering" the orbit, as Geminus apparently did. And, I suppose, this could be turned around and applied to a moving-earth theory. But the Greeks must have been reluctant to accept this lack of symmetry, and the epicycle theory did explain the observed difference in the lengths of the seasons.

The matter of the lack of parallax of the stars (that is to say, if the earth were moving, the relative positions of the stars would seem to shift) just could not be explained, because the Greeks and Romans could not accept the idea of such great distances as are actually involved. The movement of the earth is imperceptible to those who inhabit it, the distances to the stars are obviously vast, and the actual parallax is so small that it can be observed only with modern instruments.

Both explanations—the epicycle scheme of Eudoxus, Hipparchus, and Ptolemy, and the geocentric arrangement proposed by Aristarchus—were wrong in that both involved only circles rather than ellipses. In this they epitomize the handicap that was imposed on the science of the "classical" world by the rigidity of Greek mathematical thought. In general, the Greek mathematicians reasoned that natural phenomena must behave in patterns of logical regularity. Therefore the circle—that most regular of the curved figures—must certainly represent the paths of the heavenly bodies.

Indeed, natural phenomena do behave in regular ways. And these behaviors are describable in mathematical terms. But you must settle for ellipses instead of circles, and, in general, for mathematical explanations that reflect all the data and observations without prejudice, rather than preconceived mathematical theories to which the data are adapted.

You can hardly blame the Greek mathematical tradition completely for the failure of experimental science to develop —nor for the fact that technology did not develop. The fact was that neither was much needed in an economy based on slave labor. This situation did not change appreciably until the twelfth century A.D. And then mathematics began to play a significant role in a renaissance of science and technology.

10

MATHEMATICS AND EMPIRE

Clichés are tempting targets. In an era of consistent bombardment with slogans by advertising, the government, and the educational system, one must be either very gullible or very suspicious of the convenient generalization. If your inclination is toward suspicion, you will probably not stop at questioning current social clichés and might even dare to look carefully at such favorites as "Rome did not produce even one mathematician of the first rank." (In fact, most people would agree that they produced no second or third raters either.)

First, in good mathematical form, let us define terms. What is meant by "a Roman mathematician" or a "mathematician produced by Rome?" Let me note that there are people who argue that the question has no meaning, since there was no Western mathematician of stature after the time of Apollonius (ca. 225 B.C.). In so saying, they write off Diophantus, the number theorist; Pappus, whose few surviving works suggest profound insights into important geometric generalizations; Claudius Ptolemy, best known for his work in astronomy but whose mathematical ideas were probably more original than his contributions to astronomy; and others, including Hero, mentioned earlier. These men all lived in the first three centuries of the Christian era, which is certainly a Roman period.

Then you must entertain the argument that these men

were not Romans. That is, they did not carry on their mathematical activities in Rome, or even Italy. Anyone inclined toward serious study of mathematics would head for Alexandria. Alexandria was founded by Greeks—successors to Alexander the Great—but had been absorbed by Rome in the middle of the first century B.C. If these later Alexandrian mathematicians were not Roman, then were they Greek? Were, for that matter, Thales of Miletus, Apollonius of Perga, Pythagoras of Crotone, Euclid of Alexandria, Greek?

In fact, Alexandria was much more a Roman city than were many of the provincial centers. The usual Roman practice was to give towns considerable autonomy. For example, three other "Greek" towns in Egypt—Ptolemaïs, Naucratis and Antinopolis—enjoyed home rule. But Alexandria, because of the turbulence of the large and heterogeneous populace, was ruled by imperial officials.

On the other hand, the usual inclination is to call "Roman" such men as Seneca, who was Spanish—as were Quintilian and Martial—and the elder Pliny, who hailed from Cisalpine Gaul.

Perhaps many of the mathematicians of this "second Alexandrian era" were sons of Roman officials stationed in Alexandria. Of course, I have no basis upon which to make this guess; but then, so little is known about these men that there is no basis upon which to make any statement about who they were. Of Diophantus, for example, historians have argued that he lived anytime from the second century B.C.E. to the third century of the Christian era. Most agree now that the latter time is probably more accurate. (Though one of the arguments involves comparison of wine costs mentioned in some of Diophantus' problems with known rates of the era, so you can see that the reasoning is a bit obscure.) Dates of others have been established from their reports of eclipses observed.

Only fragments of the works of Hero, Pappus, and Menelaus survive—in copies—and you can hardly help but wonder how many mathematicians were obscured completely by the disasters that befell the Library at Alexandria.

Frequently cited as evidence of Roman ignorance of mathematics is the fact that there was no Latin translation of Euclid until the sixth century. But throughout the period of the principate, Greek was the language of the intellectuals. At least the educated man was as fluent in that language as he was in Latin. Marcus Aurelius, for example, wrote his *Meditations* in Greek. The apostle Paul wrote to the Romans in Greek. Greek was the language of Christian liturgy for the Church in Rome. Why translate Euclid?

Also noted, to the detriment of the Romans, was their failure to use mathematics in applied sciences—architecture, surveying, road building. I have no quarrel with this observation, though the Romans seem to have done a rather capable job using rule-of-thumb methods. I would, however, raise the question of how much of an impact "Greek" mathematics had on the nonintellectual side of Greek life, or everyday activity in Miletus, Somos, Perga, and other outlying regions.

Well, the defense rests, and I sincerely hope that these remarks will be interpreted as "in defense of the Romans" rather than as an attack on the tradition of Greek mathematics as the basis for Western developments. The latter is undebatable, though there may be need for some qualification. That there is little direct evidence for Roman qualifiers is due to the chaotic social phenomena of the time.

Some mathematics was being done at the restored academic center in Alexandria. Not so surprisingly, the mathematical work that survives from the era indicates that there was interest in the three general areas: mathematics for its own sake—pure mathematics, applied mathematics, and mathematical spin-off from the exploration of other problems—in particular those of astronomy. Of the mathematicians themselves, we have names, and practically nothing more.

Diophantus was the most original mathematician of the era—or, at least as far as is known from the works that have survived. He investigated a remarkable assortment of problems in what is now called "elementary number theory." Diophantus restricted his investigation to solutions that were rational numbers, and to this date problems that imply only rational or sometimes integral solutions are called Diophantine.

I'll give a sample of the problems Diophantus considered, in case you are inclined to this kind of thing yourself:

Book 1, Problem 30 . . . To find two numbers such that their difference and product are given numbers. ("A necessary condition," Diophantus noted, was that "Four times the product together with the square of the difference must give a square.")

Book II, Problem 9 . . . To divide a given number which is the sum of two squares into two other squares.

Book V, Problem 29 . . . To find three squares such that the sum of their squares is a square.

Diophantus, as you may have guessed from the examples, was much intrigued with square and cubic numbers in particular. This reflects the tradition of linking numerical matters with those geometric.

I mentioned earlier that Hero worked at pneumatics and mechanics, and, while his results did not always have an everyday applicability, they were nonetheless applications.

Claudius Ptolemy needed quite a bit of mathematics for his epicyclic astronomy, and, in the course of developing what he needed, wrote up the foundations of plane and spherical trigonometry. (Though much of the original work probably was done by Hipparchus.) A geometric result which still bears Ptolemy's name involves a quadrilateral inscribed in a circle. It

Claudius Ptolemy is most widely known for his misinterpretation of the earth-sun-moon-planets relationship. Apart from noting that his model served quite adequately for many hundreds of years, I submit he should be better known for his mathematical cartography. He handled the projections very nicely, indeed, and his map of the world is remarkable for the time.

was from such a device that the astronomer worked out some of his tables.

While the mathematics of Diophantus, Hero, Ptolemy, and others of this later Alexandrian era is not looked upon with particular favor by the mathematical purists, it is, nevertheless, bona fide mathematics. The social impact, however, was less than its spurious counterpart—revival of the number mysticism of the Pythagoreans and Plato.

Such a volume as *A Manual of Mathematical Knowledge Useful for an Understanding of Plato* was most likely much more widely studied than were the writings of Diophantus, for example. The *Manual* was written by Theon of Smyrna, probably in the second half of the first century A.D. and is supposed, according to the writer in his opening paragraph, to give readers who have not had training in mathematics the essentials for understanding and applying the five branches of Plato's mathematics: arithmetic, geometry, stereometry, music theory, and astronomy. There is, however, no formal treatment of geometry and stereometry, and music theory is hurried over, with emphasis on the music of the spheres and a harmonious universe. Which reduces Theon's *Manual* to a handbook on Plato's dialogue "Timaeus."

For example, here are a few lines from "Timaeus." Timaeus is expounding at considerable length about the relationship between the five regular solids and their relationship to the four elements (the fifth, the dodecahedron, "God" used in the delineation of the universe) —earth, water, fire, and air.

"To earth, then let us assign the cubical form; for earth is the most immoveable of the four and the most plastic of all bodies, and that which has the most stable bases must of necessity be of such a nature. Now, of the triangles which we assumed at first, that which has two equal sides is by nature more firmly based than that which has unequal sides; and of the compound figures which are formed out of either, the plane equilateral quadrangle has necessarily a more stable basis than the equilateral triangle, both in the whole and in parts. Wherefore, in assigning this figure to earth, we adhere to probability; and to water we assign that one of remaining forms which is the least moveable; and the most moveable of them to fire, and to air that which is intermediate. Also, we assign the smallest body to fire, and the greatest to water, and the intermediate in size to air; and, again, the acutest body to fire, and the next in acuteness to air, and the third to water."

And so it goes. If you are going to try matching the regular polyhedra with the elements, according to Plato's somewhat cryptic instructions, you might even find such a tome as Theon's *Manual* very useful indeed.

If your reaction is that the whole business is rather ridiculous, I am in complete agreement. But, apparently, many people of the time and through subsequent centuries took it seriously, which prompted the writing of a succession of "handbooks." You might compare these with the very practical handbooks written by Moslem scholars many centuries later to provide, among other things, appropriate mathematical techniques for administrators, clerks, and others concerned with government.

By contrast to the number and geometrical mysticism of "Timeaus," there is one modern note—that uncertainties about natural phenomena should be expressed in terms of probabilities. For example:

"If then, Socrates, amid the many opinions about the gods and the generation of the universe, we are not able to give notions which are altogether and in every respect exact and consistent with one another, do not be surprised. Enough, if we adduce probabilities as likely as any others: for we must remember that I who am the speaker, and you who are the judges, are only mortal men, and we ought to accept the tale which is probable and enquire no further."

I would be inclined to assign a low probability to that tale about air, fire, water, and regular polyhedra.

The Pax Romana helped make possible this second flowering of intellectual thought at Alexandria. Once Julius Caesar had re-established order in 47 B.C. when he brought in his legions at the request of the current Cleopatra (female Egyptian rulers were then customarily called "Cleopatra"; this one was the rather notorious Cleopatra immortalized by Shakespeare), the reputation of the Museum was re-established. Of course, in the civil war the Library was burned, with tremendous loss of irreplaceable manuscripts, painstakingly collected from all over the world by the far-ranging Alexandrians, who considered the Library a community project. Cleopatra did what she could to compensate for this loss by having books transferred from the library at Pergamum to Alexandria.

Alexandria, cosmopolitan center and hub of Mediterranean and Oriental trade routes, became a Roman provincial city, with the law and order this distinction carried with it. The cause of mathematics certainly benefited, though only fragments survive of the works of most mathematicians of the era. The possibility of contact with Oriental mathematics is seldom touched upon—probably because this can only be speculated upon. Rome had established trade connections with China, via both overland and sea routes. At the time of Marcus Aurelius, the empire had diplomatic representatives in China. I find the idea of exchange of mathematical ideas a likely one. (A strong case can be made for similar Chinese contact with, and influence on, the development of Indian mathematics.) For example, the rectangular co-ordinate system that Ptolemy applied to his map making had been similarly used by Chinese cartographers for centuries. Hopefully, as sources on the development of Chinese mathematics are investigated, the speculation will be confirmed, or the theory thrown out—with cause.

There is small chance of turning up significant additional

Romans carried with them their theology and religious artifacts as well as their organizational methods and techniques in construction. The heads shown here are of Mithras, a favorite Roman religious figure, discovered within the past twenty-five years in the city of London. Lower illustration is a sketch of the temple of Mithras in which the heads were found.

information in the West. As the power of imperial Rome waned, conditions in the provinces became increasingly turbulent. Alexandria, always a volatile city because of the mixed population, experienced several centuries of intermittent chaos. Civil wars were fought almost continuously, as rival claimants to the throne of Augustus pressed their claims. For example, between 235 and 285 there were twenty-six Augusti, only one of whom escaped a violent death. One emperor had to suppress eighteen rivals. Even before this period—in 215—Alexandria was plundered and the population massacred by Caracalla's troops. A revolt in Alexandria in 273 was suppressed with the usual heavy hand.

The decline of Rome is certainly well documented; the briefest of outlines should suffice here. The burden of taxation to support the vast army (as large as 400,000), welfare programs, including more and more elaborate games, and public works steadily increased and brought economic ruin to many individuals. Some of these bankrupts joined with war refugees and army deserters to form gangs of robbers, roaming at will throughout Italy and Gaul. Egypt suffered a decline in its agriculture as the irrigation system was allowed to deteriorate.

The army itself contributed to the disorder. The legions were becoming increasingly provincial, and these Germans, Britons, and Levantines did not have the pride and loyalty that characterized the legions of the earlier empire. Rival leaders sought their support, and they frequently abandoned their posts to march on Rome or wherever else civil action was in progress. The change in philosophy is very neatly summed up in the contrasting remarks of two leaders. Marcus Aurelius (ca. 170) refused soldiers' demands for a donative, saying that anything they received above and beyond the established practice would have to be wrung from the blood of their parents and relatives; Septimius Severus, thirty years later, on his deathbed, admonished his sons to "live in harmony, enrich the soldiers, and scorn all others." As the legions became increasingly preoccupied with internal conflicts, the barbarians, who had increased their pressure on the frontiers, broke through.

A Christian community had been established in Alexandria early in the first century. The new religion appealed because it offered hope for the common man—and life was bleak indeed for the common man, as the taxes increased and corrupt emperors and local officials made further demands on the citizens, including quartering troops without compensation. Christianity prospered, though during the first two centuries it assimilated many characteristics of the popular non-Christian sects, for example that of the "Great Mother."

The scholars of Alexandria continued their work amid growing pressures from the Christian community. In fact, much of the restored library was housed in the temple at Serapis. But, in the fourth century, Christianity was proclaimed the state religion of the empire, with particular strength in the eastern provinces, centered at the newly rebuilt city called Constantinople. Bitter rivalry developed between the Bishop of Rome, then becoming known as the "Pope," and the Patriarch of Constantinople. Alexandria was pressured by both factions, being bound to the eastern empire by ethnic and cultural ties and to Rome through the imperial administrators.

In 391, by order of the emperor Theodosius, the temple at Serapis was destroyed, an intentional duplication of the accidental tragedy caused by Caesar's legions. (Here, incidentally, you find a basis for demolishing another myth in the history of mathematics—that the Moslems destroyed the library. The Moslems did not arrive until 642—and even if many manuscripts survived the destruction of the temple, there must have been further drastic depletions during the next 250 years.)

In 415, Hypatia, daughter of the mathematician Theon, and herself highly regarded as a mathematician and philosopher as well as for her beauty, was murdered by a mob, incited by the Bishop of Alexandria. Her death marks the end of the second flourishing of mathematics in Alexandria.

INDEX

Sundials, Egyptian, 67
Sun worship (*see also* Ra): Incas and, 19
Supreme Inca, 15, 18, 19
Symbols, number-words represented by, 6, 26. *See also* specific kinds
Syracuse, 103–4, 109

T'ang dynasty, 28
Tao (Taoism), 25, 26, 31, 34, 39
Technology. *See* Science and technology
Temples, 43–45, 47, 55, 72, 93, 101, 115, 116, 131. *See also* Priests; Scribes; specific people, places
Ten, as magic number, 116
Tens (base ten number system), 1, 2–3, 6, 15–16, 18, 25, 32. *See also* Decimal number system
Thales, 25, 60, 82, 85–87, 88, 122
Theodosius, Emperor, 131
Theon of Smyrna, 126–27, 131
Theorems, Greeks and, 86
Thom, Alexander, 71–72
Tiahuanaco Empire, 13
Time (time-keeping), 9–10, 21–23, 67, 71 (*see also* Calendars; specific people, places); cyclic view of, 74–76; seasons and, 117–18, 120; star clock, 67; sundials, 67; water clock, 113–14
Trigonometry, 59, 124
Triples, Pythagorean, 53–54
Tsimshian Indians, 2
Twelve, as number base, 4–5
Twenty, as number base, 2–3
Two: as number base, 67;

Pythagoreans and square root of, 92

Usefulness, number systems and, 7, 9–10

Vague years. *See* Sacred and vague years, Mayan
Ventris, Michael, 76
Venus, synodic year of, 23
Vitruvius, 115–17; *De Architectura,* 115–17

Water clock, 113–14
Water supply, 114–15
Wedge-shaped tablets. *See* Cuneiform tablets
Weeping god motif, 13
Weights and measures, 32, 77
Word origins. *See* Number-words, development of
Writing, development of, 45–47 63–64, 78–79. *See also* Alphabets; Scribes; specific kinds, people, places

"Yang" and "yin," 27
Year, time-keeping and, 21–23. *See also* Calendars; Time (time-keeping)
Yu the Great, 34, 36

Zeno, 93–95; paradoxes of, 94, 95, 98
Zero, use of, 14, 20, 33, 49, 54
Zodiac, the, 67, 118
Zoser, 63
Zuñi Indians, 3, 8–9, 91, 119

MICHAEL MOFFATT is an anthropologist for whom mathematics is an avocation. A Connecticut native, he traveled back and forth across the United States while an undergraduate at Reed College in Portland, Oregon. He has done graduate work at Oxford University in England, the University of Chicago, and field work in anthropology in India. He is presently teaching at Rutgers University in New Brunswick, New Jersey.